I0112906

THE DID AND OSDD HANDBOOK

of related interest

The Simple Guide to Complex Trauma and Dissociation
What It Is and How to Help
Betsy de Thierry
Illustrated by Emma Reeves
Foreword by Graham Music
ISBN 978 1 78775 314 3
eISBN 978 1 78775 315 0

Life on Autopilot
A Guide to Living with Depersonalization Disorder
Joe Perkins
ISBN 978 1 78775 599 4
eISBN 978 1 78775 600 7

Trauma is Really Strange
Graphic Medicine
Steve Haines
Illustrated by Sophie Standing
ISBN 978 1 84819 293 5
eISBN 978 0 85701 240 1

20 Ways to Break Free From Trauma
From Brain Hijacking to Post-Traumatic Growth
Philippa Smethurst
Foreword by Sir Terry Waite, KCMG CBE
ISBN 978 1 80501 310 5
eISBN 978 1 80501 311 2

Talking About BPD
A Stigma-Free Guide to Living a Calmer, Happier
Life with Borderline Personality Disorder
Rosie Cappuccino
Foreword by Kimberley Wilson
ISBN 978 1 78775 825 4
eISBN 978 1 78775 826 1
Audio ISBN 978 1 52937 104 8

The DID and OSDD Handbook

Understanding *and* Navigating Life *with* Dissociative Identity Disorder

ELLA EVERETT

Foreword by Dr Adrian A. Fletcher

Jessica Kingsley Publishers
London and Philadelphia

First published in Great Britain in 2026 by Jessica Kingsley Publishers
An imprint of John Murray Press

2

Copyright © Ella Everett 2026
Foreword copyright © Dr Adrian A. Fletcher 2026

The right of Ella Everett to be identified as the Author of the Work has been asserted by them in accordance with the Copyright, Designs and Patents Act 1988.

Front cover image illustrated by Ella Everett. The cover image is for illustrative purposes only.

All rights reserved. No part of this publication may be reproduced, stored in a retrieval system, or transmitted, in any form or by any means without the prior written permission of the publisher, nor be otherwise circulated in any form of binding or cover other than that in which it is published and without a similar condition being imposed on the subsequent purchaser.

The information contained in this book is not intended to replace the services of trained medical professionals or to be a substitute for medical advice. You are advised to consult a doctor on any matters relating to your health, and in particular on any matters that may require diagnosis or medical attention.

Content warning: Topics that the reader may find triggering include different types of trauma, suicide, self-harm and intimacy.

A CIP catalogue record for this title is available from the British Library and the Library of Congress

ISBN 978 1 83997 558 5
eISBN 978 1 83997 559 2

Printed and bound in the United States by Integrated Books International

Jessica Kingsley Publishers' policy is to use papers that are natural, renewable and recyclable products and made from wood grown in sustainable forests. The logging and manufacturing processes are expected to conform to the environmental regulations of the country of origin.

Jessica Kingsley Publishers
Carmelite House
50 Victoria Embankment
London EC4Y 0DZ

www.jkp.com

John Murray Press
Part of Hodder & Stoughton Ltd
An Hachette Company

The authorised representative in the EEA is Hachette Ireland,
8 Castlecourt Centre, Dublin 15, D15 XTP3, Ireland (email: info@hbgi.ie)

*To our beautiful family, thank you for
your continuous love and support.*

*To those with DID and OSDD, may your
journey be as peaceful as possible.*

Acknowledgements

We extend our heartfelt thanks to every individual with DID and OSDD who has shared their experiences with us, as well as to the wider online system community. We are deeply grateful to all of those who have offered support to people with DID and OSDD, including medical, mental health and support professionals who continue to provide care and understanding. Our appreciation also goes to the researchers, past and present, who have dedicated their work to the study of trauma and multiplicity.

We would like to sincerely thank everyone involved in the creation of this book. We are especially grateful to the team at JKP for their invaluable support throughout the publishing process and for providing us with the opportunity to raise awareness of DID and OSDD. A special thanks to Jane, Carys and Will.

We are also thankful to Jacq A for their thoughtful review and important contributions to the 'BIPOC Systems' and 'Intersectionality' sections of this book. We are grateful for the support we have received in therapy that has helped guide us through important stages of our recovery.

Finally, we extend our warmest thanks to our friends and family. Your acceptance, kindness and unwavering support have meant the world to us. Without you, this book would not have been possible.

Contents

PART 4: SYSTEMS IN SOCIETY AND THE MEDIA

PART 5: GETTING HELP

Disclaimer

Each person on this earth is unique, no two people are the same. The same goes for people with DID and OSDD, everyone is different. This means that not everything written in this book will be applicable to everyone with DID and OSDD. In terms of OSDD, this book focuses on OSDD sub-type 1, which refers to people with OSDD who have multiple alters.

This book is not just based on our personal experiences as a person with DID. It has been informed by the experiences of people with DID and OSDD all over the world, and it therefore aims to be a representative experience of what it is like to navigate life with these conditions.

As a white British person with DID, we acknowledge our biases and privileges.

We are not a mental health professional but an expert by experience, with a diagnosis of DID. This book is not intended to replace the services of trained medical professionals or to be a substitute for medical advice. You are advised to consult a doctor or mental health professional on any matters relating to your health, and in particular on any matters that may require diagnosis or medical attention.

The scientific research, studies and articles referenced in the book are the most up to date at the time of writing; however, over time, future studies will be published which will likely reveal more data on DID and OSDD.

Other people have been referenced in this book including mental health professionals and well-known multiples. We are independent, not connected with them and therefore do not endorse their views or opinions.

Content warning: This book includes topics that some readers may find triggering, such as various forms of trauma, suicide, self-harm and intimacy. If you do not feel comfortable or stable enough, we recommend that you skip these sections.

A Note on Language

People with DID and OSDD may use different words to describe their separate 'identities'. Examples include but are not limited to: alters, parts, headmates, system mates, personas, identities, personalities, alternate personalities, members, people, self states, others, fragments, roommates, friends and selves. This book uses the word 'alters' as, in our experience, this is the most commonly used term worldwide in the DID and OSDD community.

People with DID and OSDD may also use different words to describe the *collection* of their alters. Examples include but are not limited to: system, multiple, plural, collective, person with DID/OSDD, pwDID, pwOSDD, unity, community, all of me, family, team, assembly, the others, squad and group. This book uses the word 'system' as, in our experience, this is the most commonly used term worldwide in the DID and OSDD community.

Throughout the book, we as the author give insights and examples of how DID manifests for us. Here we use the plural pronoun 'we' which refers to everyone in our system collectively.

It is up to each person with DID and OSDD to decide which words they would like to use to describe their experience. Some may decide not to use any. If people with DID and OSDD do not want to use some/all of the vocabulary in this book that is completely fine.

Those who work with systems such as therapists and those who work in the mental health field may also use different words for 'alters' and 'system'.

Some other terms in this book may have been coined by the DID and OSDD community because there was a need for new vocabulary to help explain their experience. Some of these terms may not be found in academic literature but that does not erase the need for them, their prevalence or their importance.

Foreword

"Show love and respect to all your parts and those parts will likely come to love and respect all of you."

DR ADRIAN A. FLETCHER

I, Dr Adrian A. Fletcher, member of the BlenDID System, first came to know Ella and their work through Instagram via @dissociation. info. Before I/we decided to come forward publicly with our own lived experience of dissociative identity disorder (DID) their Instagram account provided such solace and validation to what I was experiencing amongst my own system of PARTs. They provided me with information that even myself at times had not yet come to know or understand and for that I was and am extremely grateful. It can be an isolating journey to live life with a dissociative condition and extremely challenging to heal from the atrocities done to us that created these conditions in the first place. Please know that you are not alone in your experience if you live with DID. An estimated 1–3 per cent of the population is living with DID and many suspect that those numbers are much higher.

Life for those with dissociative identity disorder (DID) and otherwise specified dissociative disorder (OSDD) is fraught with a great deal of complexity and pain. As a human and professional psychologist living with DID, my own system of PARTs has waited years for a book like this one. Dissociative disorders are unfortunately highly stigmatised and misunderstood. Those of us living with these conditions on the path to healing are often on a deep search to find answers and help to better understand our dissociative systems of alters/parts.

Ella has provided us with a simple to understand guide. The information shared with us is delivered in a clear, kind and compassionate way that few others can offer us as a population of people living with DID. They have devoted their time and energy to serving the community at large with education we have not been able to easily locate elsewhere and for that there are not enough words to express the immense gratitude we have for this book.

This guidebook can be used as a template and framework for individuals that live with OSDD and DID. Some people living with these conditions refer to their parts as a dissociative system or DID system and each person with these conditions and their system of parts will need to decide what aspects of this guidebook apply to them and which ones do not. It is important to use discernment when navigating the content of this guidebook. You and your parts get to decide what resonates and what does not.

I could not be more honoured to continue to support Ella and all that they do to help us all create our own unique paths to healing. I hope you and your system of parts enjoy this guidebook as much as I/we do. Be gentle with yourselves on the path to healing. All parts of you and your system deserve love, kindness, compassion and respect. Remember to take things one moment, one day at a time. May you be guided and inspired to create the life you desire and deserve. Please don't give up. The world needs you(s).

Warmly,

Dr Adrian A. Fletcher/BlenDID System
Multilayered Human First
Psychologist Second

Preface

Life with DID and OSDD is not always easy. It can feel lonely, confusing, exhausting and difficult. This book intends to help the reader by providing detailed information on DID and OSDD, allowing systems to feel less alone in their struggles, better understand their experiences and learn how to best help themselves. It covers specific topics that academic books often overlook and uses simple language to make the concepts more accessible. The book also aims to provide an insight into what life with DID and OSDD is like, aims to help support and educate those who know people with DID and OSDD and includes tips for those who know and work with systems.

Dissociative identity disorder (DID) and other specified dissociative disorder (OSDD) are highly stigmatised mental health conditions. There is a lack of knowledge about DID and OSDD in society, the media and even among some mental healthcare professionals. The misunderstanding and misrepresentation of these conditions can make life more difficult for people with DID and OSDD. DID and OSDD systems are not rare, they do not have evil alters and they are not criminals. They are simply people who have experienced childhood trauma.

People with DID and OSDD deserve to be understood and treated with kindness. We hope that one day everyone with DID and OSDD gets the recognition, representation and help that they all deserve.

This book compiles a plethora of information, covering all you need to know about DID and OSDD (sub-type 1). If you do not know anything about DID and OSDD or only know a little, it might be beneficial to read it in order, starting with *What Are DID and OSDD?*. Otherwise, the book can be dipped into at any point. We encourage you to take your time while navigating through the book.

The book is split into six parts:

* **Part 1: What Are DID and OSDD?** We begin with an in-depth look at what DID and OSDD are, why, how and when they form. We then explore the difference between DID and OSDD, the prevalence, the history and debunk the common myths. Following this, we look at the theory, the brain, the types of trauma which cause these conditions, system size and alter types.

* **Part 2: Living with DID and OSDD** Part 2 explores the intricacies of what it is like to live with DID and OSDD. This includes: all about switching and fronting, co-consciousness, all about littles, making alter profiles, fusion, splitting and inner worlds. We then look at multiplicity around the world, 'coming out' as a system, system mapping and communication, remembering trauma, manifestations of trauma and intersectionality.

* **Part 3: Navigating the World** This part looks at how to navigate work and school as a system, how to navigate friendships, dating, intimacy, parenthood, inner system relationships and how to cope in medical situations.

* **Part 4: Systems in Society and the Media** Part 4 discusses multiplicity in the media, the stigma, well-known systems, fakeclaiming and the system community.

* **Part 5: Getting Help** Here we explore the process of getting an assessment and diagnosis, misdiagnosis, social and philosophical perspectives, 'final' fusion and functional

multiplicity. We then look at psychiatric hospitals, how to manage a mental health crisis and additional ways systems can help themselves.

- ◆ **Part 6: Supporting Systems** This final section looks at how friends, family, partners, therapists and mental health professionals can support systems. It also explores how to talk to systems, how to help in a crisis and looks at what can be done to help prevent future childhood trauma.

The book ends with an extensive list of resources and recommended organisations, as well as a DID and OSDD Dictionary of Terminology.

PART 1

What Are DID and OSDD?

CHAPTER 1

An Introduction to DID and OSDD

Definitions of Diagnoses

+ **DID** stands for dissociative identity disorder.

+ **OSDD** stands for other specified disscociative disorder.

+ **MPD** stands for multiple personality disorder. This is the old diagnostic name for DID. MPD changed to DID in 1994 in the Diagnostic and Statistical Manual of Mental Disorders (DSM).[1]

+ **DDNOS** stands for dissociative disorder not otherwise specified. This is the old diagnostic name for OSDD. DDNOS changed to OSDD in 2013.[2] The OSDD diagnostic criteria are more specific and structured compared to the DDNOS criteria.

DID and OSDD are mental health conditions. DID and OSDD are the most complex dissociative disorders. People develop DID and OSDD due to experiencing childhood trauma.

People with DID and OSDD sub-type 1 have distinct identities known as parts or alters, which are dissociated parts of one mind. They share the same body but have different ways of experiencing the world. These alters can differ in age, gender and personality. They can also have different interests, thoughts and emotions. The term *system* is often used to describe the collection of alters. Alters can take turns controlling the body. People with DID and OSDD experience dissociation, derealisation, depersonalisation, severe amnesia, identity alteration and identity confusion. Identity alteration refers to having different alters who may take control of the body at different times, while identity confusion refers to struggles with self-perception and maintaining a continuous sense of self.

People who do not have DID or OSDD may be referred to by some as 'non-systems' (as used in this book for ease) or 'singlets'.

The Diagnostic Criteria

The diagnostic criteria for dissociative disorders can be found in The Diagnostic and Statistical Manual of Mental Disorders, 5th Edition (DSM-5) and the International Classification of Diseases, 11th Revision (ICD-11). The DSM-5 lists the diagnostic criteria for DID and OSDD. The DSM-5 can be purchased online and is available to read in some libraries. The ICD-11 lists the diagnostic criteria for DID and P-DID and can be viewed on the ICD-11 website.

The DID Diagnostic Criteria

The DID criteria in the ICD-11 is as follows:

> Dissociative identity disorder is characterised by disruption of identity in which there are two or more distinct personality states (dissociative identities) associated with marked discontinuities in the sense of self and agency. Each personality state includes its own pattern of experiencing, perceiving, conceiving, and relating to self, the body and the environment. At least two distinct personality states recurrently take executive control of the individual's consciousness and functioning in interacting with others or with the environment, such as in the performance of specific aspects of daily life such as parenting, or work, or in response to specific

situations (e.g., those that are perceived as threatening). Changes in personality state are accompanied by related alterations in sensation, perception, affect, cognition, memory, motor control and behaviour. There are typically episodes of amnesia, which may be severe. The symptoms are not better explained by another mental, behavioural or neurodevelopmental disorder and are not due to the direct effects of a substance or medication on the central nervous system, including withdrawal effects, and are not due to a disease of the nervous system or a sleep-wake disorder. The symptoms result in significant impairment in personal, family, social, educational occupational or other important areas of functioning.[3]

For more information about DID diagnostic criteria, you can also refer to the DSM-5.

The Difference between DID and OSDD

In OSDD-1, people almost meet the criteria for DID; however, their alters may be less distinct and/or they do not experience the severe dissociative amnesia required for a DID diagnosis.

The OSDD Diagnostic Criteria (The Different Sub-Types)

The OSDD diagnosis is used when the full criteria for the other dissociative disorders are not met and a specific reason is provided for this. In the DSM-5, the OSDD diagnosis is divided into four categories, which are summarised below. For the full diagnostic criteria please refer to the DSM-5.

1. Long term, persistent and recuring symptoms of dissociation. This involves a disruption of identity, such as a lack of integration between self and abilities, changes in sense of self or experiences of possession, without evidence of dissociative amnesia.

2. Disruption of identity resulting from extreme long-term coercive persuasion, such as torture or brainwashing. This

can include long-lasting alternations in identity or question-ing one's sense of self.

3. Severe dissociative responses to high stress incidents. These usually last for days, hours or less than a month. They may involve reduced awareness, perceptual distortions, tempo-rary amnesia, derealisation, depersonalisation, temporary stupor or changes in sensory-motor ability.

4. Dissociative trance, which involves a total lack of awareness of the nearby environment, often appearing as deep unre-sponsiveness to external stimulation. Minor repetitive move-ments or vocalisations may be present. The individual may lose consciousness or experience temporary paralysis. These symptoms are not better explained by recognised spiritual or cultural customs.

The OSDD sub-type 1 (OSDD-1) is informally divided by the com-munity into OSDD-1a and OSDD-1b. **OSDD-1a** refers to people who experience dissociation and identity disturbance but do not have fully distinct alters or do not fully alternate between them. People with OSDD-1a may not have different names for their alters, instead, their alters may present as different versions or ages of the same person. They may experience more blending and co-con-sciousness and switching may feel more subtle.

OSDD-1b refers to people who have clearly distinct alters, similar to those seen in DID, and they may fully switch between them. However, people with OSDD-1b do not experience disso-ciative amnesia between their alters, which is required for a DID diagnosis. This means people with OSDD-1b are aware of what happens when other alters front and generally retain memory when switching. Some OSDD systems may refer to their sub-type, while others may not.

Some people with OSDD may feel less valid than those with

DID, because the DID diagnosis is widely known. However, as stated in *Dissociation and the Dissociative Disorders: DSM-V and Beyond*:[4] 'studies have consistently found that 40% of diagnosed dissociative disorders are DDNOS'. (DDNOS is the old diagnostic name for OSDD.)

The Partial DID Diagnostic Criteria

Partial dissociative identity disorder (P-DID) is a more recent diagnosis (2022) that is present in the International Classification of Diseases (ICD-11). It is most similar to OSDD-1. The P-DID criteria in the ICD-11 is as follows:

Partial dissociative identity disorder is characterised by disruption of identity in which there are two or more distinct personality states (dissociative identities) associated with marked discontinuities in the sense of self and agency. Each personality state includes its own pattern of experiencing, perceiving, conceiving and relating to self, the body and the environment. One personality state is dominant and normally functions in daily life, but is intruded upon by one or more non-dominant personality states (dissociative intrusions). These intrusions may be cognitive, affective, perceptual, motor or behavioural. They are experienced as interfering with the functioning of the dominant personality state and are typically aversive. The non-dominant personality states do not recurrently take executive control of the individual's consciousness and functioning, but there may be occasional, limited and transient episodes in which a distinct personality state assumes executive control to engage in circumscribed behaviours, such as in response to extreme emotional states or during episodes of self-harm or the reenactment of traumatic memories. The symptoms are not better explained by another mental, behavioural or neurodevelopmental disorder and are not due to the direct effects of a substance or medication on the central nervous system, including withdrawal effects, and are not due to a disease of the nervous system or a sleep-wake disorder. The symptoms result in significant impairment in personal, family, social, educational, occupational or other important areas of functioning.[5]

How Common Are DID and OSDD?

It is often assumed that DID and OSDD are rare conditions; however, this is not the case. It is generally estimated that at least 1–3 per cent of the population have DID or OSDD. According to The International Society for the Study of Trauma and Dissociation (ISSTD), 'DID and dissociative disorders are not rare conditions. In studies of the general population, a prevalence rate of DID of 1% to 3% of the population has been described.'[6]

The DSM-5, states the prevalence of DID as 1.5 per cent.[7] This suggests that DID and OSDD are likely just as common, if not more common, than schizophrenia and obsessive-compulsive disorder (OCD). The DSM-5 states the prevalence of OCD as 1.2 per cent[8] and the prevalence of schizophrenia as 0.3 per cent to 0.7 per cent.[9] The DSM-5 does not list a prevalence rate for OSDD.

Prevalence rates provide an estimate of how common a condition is within a population. The article 'Dissociative identity disorder: Out of the shadows at last?' states that 'DID has an estimated lifetime prevalence of around 1.5% meaning that at least one million people in the UK will suffer from DID during their life'.[10] The United Nations stated the world's population in 2022 as 8 billion. That means in 2022 there were at least 120 million systems worldwide.[11]

The prevalence rates of DID and OSDD have also been looked at in college populations. A meta-analysis study reviewed 31,905 college students across 12 studies that specifically diagnosed dissociative disorders. They found that 'the prevalence rate for DDNOS was 4.5%' (now called OSDD) and 'the prevalence rate for DID was 3.7%'.[12]

The prevalence of DID and OSDD appears to be even higher in both inpatient and outpatient psychiatric settings. The book

Dissociative Identity Disorder: Treatment and Management states the prevalence of DID in psychiatric inpatient settings as a median of 5 per cent[13] and the prevalence of DID in psychiatric outpatient settings as a median of 2.5 per cent.[14]

Research also shows that females are approximately nine times more likely than males to be diagnosed with DID.[15] This may be partly be because girls are more likely to experience child sexual abuse than boys. The CDC states that 'one in four girls and one in 20 boys in the United States experience child sexual abuse'.[16] Both sets of data exclude people who do not identify as female or male.

There is more data on the prevalence of DID than OSDD. The prevalence of DID *and* OSDD systems is likely to be higher in studies where only DID has been documented. Data from studies also often only includes the prevalence rates of *diagnosed* systems, so the true prevalence is likely to be higher when undiagnosed systems are also considered. Different studies and articles show slight variations in their findings on the prevalence of DID and OSDD. However, most suggest a prevalence rate of at least 1 per cent. Future research will continue to help give further insight and clarification.

Why and How DID and OSDD Form

DID and OSDD develop as a result of childhood trauma. They are the brain's clever protective and adaptive coping mechanisms in response to childhood trauma. Developing DID and OSDD is not dysfunctional, it allows a traumatised child to survive and function in everyday life. Not everyone who has childhood trauma will develop DID or OSDD. However, everyone with DID and OSDD has experienced childhood trauma.

The trauma is compartmentalised and amnesia walls in the brain prevent the child from consciously remembering the traumatic experiences and their identity becomes dissociated into different alters. This allows the child to continue living a 'normal' life without awareness of the trauma. More trauma or difficulty in childhood can result in the creation of more alters to help cope.

DID can be understood through the developmental trauma model,[17] which proposes that the personality develops as a collection of self-states that never fully integrate during childhood. Alternatively, the older theory of structural dissociation describes DID as the personality separating into distinct alters.

Part, Alter or Personality?

Different mental health professionals and systems refer to the dissociated selves differently. Some people use the term 'alters' while others call them 'parts'. Both terms refer to the same principle. Systems may have a preference for which word is used to refer to their alters, as may professionals.

+ **Part** is the term used in the theory of structural dissociation and in the Internal Family Systems model of psychotherapy.

+ **Alter** is short for alternate identity or personality state and is sometimes referred to as an alternate state of reality or consciousness.

+ **Personality** is generally no longer used, now that it is understood that each alter is not a separate personality but part of one whole personality, that did not fully form to become one.

Some systems may use other words to refer to their separate states of identity, such as headmates, identities, personas, people, others, system mates or members.

TIPS FOR SUPPORTING PEOPLE WITH DID AND OSDD
Use the language preferred by the system you know, such as the term they use to refer to their alters.

What Is Dissociation?

We all – systems and non-systems – dissociate. Have you ever realised that you were staring off into space and wondered where you had gone? You were dissociating. It can be described as floating away from reality or zoning out. Dissociation is a survival mechanism. It is one of the brain's responses to stress and trauma. It is detaching from the present. People with dissociative disorders experience dissociation more frequently and more severely than those without. It can also greatly impact their lives. Dissociation is very common for DID and OSDD systems, and although it happens subconsciously, it can create a sense of safety. Dissociation was helpful for systems enduring trauma; it helped them survive. For systems, dissociation becomes a learned response to stress, meaning that when they are no longer in danger, dissociation can get in the way of everyday life.

Dissociation exists on a spectrum, ranging from everyday experiences like daydreaming to severe and chronic dissociation present in dissociative disorders. This diagram shows how dissociation can be seen in different conditions, from mild to extreme.

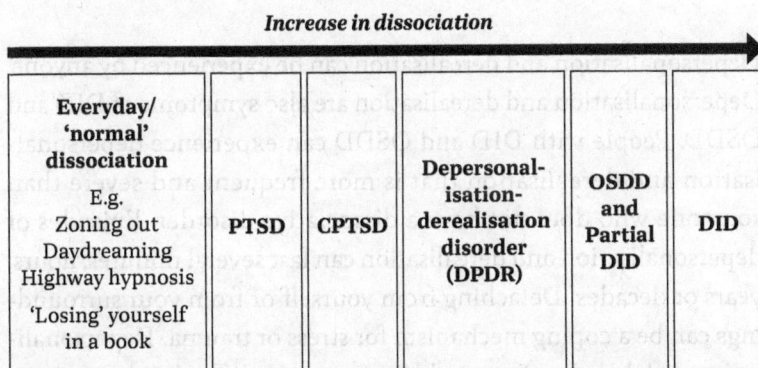

Increase in dissociation

→

Everyday/ 'normal' dissociation E.g. Zoning out Daydreaming Highway hypnosis 'Losing' yourself in a book	PTSD	CPTSD	Depersonal- isation- derealisation disorder (DPDR)	OSDD and Partial DID	DID

DISSOCIATION AS A SPECTRUM

What Can Dissociating Feel Like?

+ Your mind feels blurry.
+ Your body feels floaty.

- Your mind goes blank.
- Your thoughts feel fuzzy.
- Your brain fills with static.
- Your vision becomes unfocused, like a camera.
- You feel like you are in a fog.
- You feel unreal.
- You feel like you are on another planet.
- Your mind feels paused.
- You cannot comprehend your surroundings.
- You feel like you are falling asleep.

Depersonalisation and Derealisation

- **Depersonalisation** is feeling detached from yourself, your body or feeling that you are not real.

- **Derealisation** is feeling that the world is distorted, distant or not real.

Depersonalisation and derealisation can be experienced by anyone. Depersonalisation and derealisation are also symptoms of DID and OSDD. People with DID and OSDD can experience depersonalisation and derealisation that is more frequent and severe than someone who does not have a dissociative disorder. Episodes of depersonalisation and derealisation can last several minutes, hours, years or decades. Detaching from yourself or from your surroundings can be a coping mechanism for stress or trauma. Depersonalisation and derealisation can feel very surreal, difficult to experience and hard to describe.

Symptoms of depersonalisation include:

- not feeling real
- feeling like a robot

+ feeling like your body is not your own
+ feeling like you are floating outside of your body
+ feeling like you are watching yourself in a film or from a bird's eye view
+ not recognising your reflection in a mirror
+ your limbs feeling distorted, such as feeling too big or too small
+ feeling physically or emotionally numb
+ viewing your thoughts, behaviours and emotions from a distance
+ your memories not feeling like your own.

Symptoms of derealisation include:

+ feeling like the world is not real
+ feeling like you are in a dream or film
+ feeling detached from your surroundings or finding them unfamiliar or foggy
+ your sense of time being distorted
+ objects looking distorted, such as looking the wrong shape or size
+ feeling disconnected from people you know or them feeling unreal.

For information on how to cope with depersonalisation and derealisation, see Chapter 15.

Dissociative Disorders

Dissociative disorders are a group of mental health conditions involving dissociation. People are diagnosed with a dissociative disorder when their symptoms significantly effect their everyday life. You can still have a dissociative disorder even without a formal diagnosis.

The dissociative disorders are:

- **Dissociative identity disorder (DID)**

- **Other specified dissociative disorder (OSDD)**

- **Partial DID**

- **Depersonalisation-derealisation disorder (DPDR):** Is experiencing frequent depersonalisation and/or derealisation which impacts your daily life. It is a separate diagnosis from DID and OSDD. It does not involve distinct alters. DID and OSDD systems can also experience depersonalisation and derealisation.

- **Dissociative amnesia:** Difficulty remembering parts of your past or personal information about yourself. Systems can also experience this. Dissociative amnesia with fugue is a sub-type of dissociative amnesia. This is when someone finds themselves in a place that they do not recognise, have no recollection as to how they got there and may not remember some or all of their past. This can be a frightening experience. Systems can also experience this.

- **Unspecified dissociative disorder (UDD):** This diagnosis may be given when someone's symptoms do not fully meet the criteria for the other dissociative disorders, such as in an emergency situation. A mental health professional may not have enough information to give a full diagnosis or decides not to specify why someone does not meet the criteria for the other diagnoses. Systems can be given this diagnosis. UDD systems may be given a diagnosis of DID or OSDD at a later date.

The History of DID

There are many examples of DID throughout history. The book *Dissociative Identity Disorder: Treatment and Management* states the 'history of dissociative identity disorder might be traced back to Palaeolithic cave paintings portraying shamans'.[18] This suggests that the potential to develop DID could have always been part of the human experience. The article 'Separating fact from fiction: An empirical examination of six myths about dissociative identity disorder' states that 'DID cases have been described in the literature for hundreds of years' and 'the first published cases are those of Jeanne Fery, reported in 1586, and a case of "exchanged personality" that dates to Eberhardt Gmelin's account of 1791'. DID is not a modern occurrence, the only difference is the language used to describe the experience. The article also states that 'many of the individuals considered hysterics in the nineteenth century would today be diagnosed with dissociative disorders'.[19] Recognising the history of DID can help validate the experiences and existence of systems today.

CHAPTER 2

Debunking the Myths

Unfortunately, many inaccuracies exist when it comes to people's assumptions about DID and OSDD. Here, some of the most common myths are debunked.

Myth: DID and OSDD Are Not Real

This is false. The UK Rare Diseases Framework states that 'a rare disease is defined as a condition which affects less than 1 in 2,000 people'.[1] It may seem like a difficult concept to comprehend, that multiple alters can exist in one body, but it is possible. The creation of alters is an adaptive coping mechanism in response to childhood trauma. Everyone dissociates and DID and OSDD are just a more chronic and complex form of dissociation. DID and OSDD are both listed in the DSM-5 and ICD-11 as mental health disorders and are only diagnosed by trained mental health professionals. Brain scans have also shown evidence of alters switching and systems exist all over the world. Research has challenged the idea that people with DID are simply pretending. Psychophysiological and neurobiological differences were found between people with DID and healthy controls who were instructed to pretend they had DID.[2]

Myth: You Will Know If You Are a System

This is false. You may have DID or OSDD but not yet know you have it. This is due to dissociative amnesia, which protects systems from knowing about their trauma and other alters, allowing them to get on with everyday life.

Myth: DID and OSDD Are Rare

This is false. The UK Rare Diseases Framework states that 'a rare disease is defined as a condition which affects less than 1 in 2,000 people'. At least 1 in 100 people in the world has DID or OSDD,[3] this means DID and OSDD are not rare. This is a lot of people. The United Nations stated the world's population in 2022 as 8 billion. That means in 2022 there were at least 120 million systems worldwide.[4]

Myth: People with DID or OSDD Have an Evil Alter or Are Criminals

This is false. People with DID or OSDD are no more likely to be dangerous than the average person. They are actually more likely to be the victim of a crime than the perpetrator of one.[5] The book *Dissociative Identity Disorder: Treatment and Management* states 'no criminal association or link is found with DID'.[6] The film *Split*[7] is about someone with DID who has 'evil' alters. This is a cinematic trope used to create an 'interesting' storyline. The film is widely criticised for its inaccurate and stigmatising portrayal of DID. Systems do not have 'evil' alters.

Myth: People with DID or OSDD Are Possessed

This is false. This interpretation was made in the past before much was known about mental illness and trauma. It may still be prevalent in some communities today, such as within some religious communities. However, contemporary research, neuroscience, psychology and clinical practice all recognise DID and OSDD as mental health conditions and not as possession.

Myth: DID and OSDD Are Personality Disorders

This is a common misconception and is false. DID and OSDD belong to a group of mental health conditions called dissociative disorders, which is a separate and different category to personality disorders.

Myth: You Can Tell if Someone Is a DID or OSDD System

This is false. Multiplicity is only obvious in around 6 per cent of systems who present more overtly.[8] The myth that all systems are visibly identifiable creates a false narrative which can lead to biases.

Myth: Childhood Trauma Always Takes Place in the Home/Family

This is false. Some systems have trauma related to their home or family, others have trauma from outside those settings and some may not have trauma connected to home or family at all. Some systems have loving and supportive families, and aside from their trauma, may have had a good childhood.

Myth: DID and OSDD Systems Are 'Crazy' or 'Insane'

This is false. Calling people who have a mental health condition or who differ from the 'norm' 'crazy' or 'insane' is derogatory and perpetuates mental health stigma. Using these as a slur is ableist, discriminatory, demeaning and offensive. This language is harmful as it can prevent systems from seeking help. Systems are not 'crazy', their brains have simply adapted to survive childhood trauma.

Myth: It Must Be Fun Being a System – You Are Never Lonely Because of Alters Sharing One Body

This is false. Systems can feel lonely. They may not know anyone else who is a system, making them feel different and alienated. For some, their alters may never talk to each other, hear each other or see each other (in their inner world). Even alters who can communicate with each other can still feel lonely. Having alters does not prevent loneliness. Sharing a body can also be complex and life as a system is more than sharing a body. Alters are formed because of trauma and there is nothing fun about that. Some alters in a system may not get on with each other, be very different to each other or want different things, whether day to day or in life. Systems can have inner system conflict. However, some systems do find it comforting and nice to be able to communicate with their alters but this is not an antidote to loneliness.

Myth: DID Is Only Recognised in Countries Where English Is the First Language

This is false. The article 'Separating fact from fiction: An empirical examination of six myths about dissociative identity disorder'[9] states that a 'study assessed the treatment outcome of 232 DID patients from around the world' and 'the participants came from every continent except Antarctica'. The countries included were 'Argentina, Australia, Belgium, Brazil, Canada, Germany, Israel, the Netherlands, New Zealand, Norway, Singapore, Slovakia, South Africa, Sweden, Taiwan, and the United States'.

TIPS FOR SUPPORTING PEOPLE WITH DID AND OSDD
Avoid using the words 'crazy' or 'mad' when referring to systems and people with mental health conditions; they are not 'crazy' or 'mad'. The language you use matters.

CHAPTER 3

The Theory

The Theory of Structural Dissociation

The theory of structural dissociation was developed by Onno Van Der Hart, Ellert R.S. Nijenhuis and Kathy Steele.[1] It refers to the dissociation and fragmentation of the personality as a result of trauma. The theory is applicable to all trauma related conditions. The theory is split into primary, secondary and tertiary structural dissociation. Tertiary structural dissociation refers to dissociative identity disorder, where the personality is divided into multiple parts, in order to survive. Extreme stress can activate the trauma defences, such as fight or flight. Structural dissociation explains that the responses to trauma can become compartmentalised, resulting in the division of the personality and therefore different alters. The theory is a framework for clinicians and mental health professionals to understand and treat those with childhood trauma, including people with DID and OSDD. The structural dissociation theory assumes that the personality was whole to start with, then split. However, there are now newer models which suggest alternative theories, such as Loewenstein positing that because the personality was not yet fully formed in early development, it never became whole to begin with, and therefore could not split. Loewenstein states 'DID is more like a never-assembled psychological jigsaw puzzle, not a shattered mirror'.[2]

Trauma Responses

Trauma responses are the ways in which people automatically and instinctively react to overwhelming threat in order to survive. These responses can be triggered by a physical or psychological threat, such as stress, fear or trauma. People do not consciously choose how they respond. The trauma responses can also show up as different behaviours and coping strategies. The six most commonly recognised trauma responses are:

- **Fight** means resisting or fighting against what is happening. Behaviours include feeling angry, being aggressive or standing up for yourselves.

- **Flight** means running away, avoiding or hiding from what is happening. Behaviours include fleeing, hiding or always keeping constantly busy.

- **Freeze** means your body freezing and being unable to move. This is a common response to sexual abuse and is not a form of consent. Behaviours include feeling numb, overwhelmed or dissociating.

- **Flop** means submitting and becoming limp or unresponsive, such as passing out. It is similar to the freeze response and resembles an animal playing dead. Behaviours include feeling hopeless, disoriented or shutting down.

- **Fawn** means giving in, appeasing or complying with what is happening to try to keep yourself safe. Behaviours include engaging in people pleasing, avoiding conflict or abandoning your own needs.

- **Friend** means trying to find someone else to help with what is happening, such as crying out for a bystander or trying to 'befriend' the perpetrator. Behaviours include feeling helpless or seeking protection from others.

For people with DID and OSDD, trauma responses can become sub-consciously learned behaviours, meaning that they can impact them for years after their trauma, even into adulthood and long after they are no longer in danger. Different alters can also be stuck in different trauma responses. Systems can have fight parts, flight parts, freeze parts, flop parts, fawn parts and friend parts. This means that multiple trauma responses can be experienced at the same time in a system, which can feel confusing and contradictory.

The Window of Tolerance

The term window of tolerance was coined by Dr Dan Siegel in 1999.[3] It describes the optimal zone of arousal which allows people to function effectively day to day. Within the window of tolerance people can think rationally, regulate their emotions and manage challenges. This zone represents a balance between hyperarousal and hypoarousal.

Hyperarousal	Window of Tolerance	Hypoarousal
Hypervigilance	Rational	Depression
Anxiety and fear	Stable and calm	Low energy or fatigue
Panic	Safe	Social isolation
Problems with sleeping	Present and alert	Feeling emotionally numb
Problems concentrating	Empathetic	Hopelessness
Anger	Curious	Dissociation
Self-harm	Engaged	Depersonalisation
Engaging in risky behaviours	Can problem solve	Derealisation
Fight and flight response	Can balance emotion and reason	Freeze and flop response

People with DID and OSDD may have some alters who engage in hyperarousal behaviours and others who engage in hypoarousal behaviours. Systems may feel ashamed of their behaviours such as self-harming. Learning that these behaviours are in fact trauma responses may help reduce self-blame.

Multiplicity and the Brain

Neuroscience has shed light on how the brain reacts to trauma. Trauma can physically change the brain through a variety of neural, chemical and structural processes. While trauma related brain changes can be seen in PTSD, CPTSD, OSDD and DID, DID and OSDD exhibit additional and more complex alterations in brain function and structure. In childhood, the brain develops differently in people with DID and OSDD than in those without these conditions. Multiple scientific studies have investigated how DID affects the brain structure and function. The article 'Separating fact from fiction: An empirical examination of six myths about dissociative identity disorder' states that 'DID patients can be differentiated from other psychiatric patients, healthy controls, and DID simulators in neurophysiological and psychological research'.[4]

The article 'Dissociative identity disorder: An empirical overview' summarised many studies regarding DID and the brain. The article stated 'significant functional brain imaging (PET and fMRI) differences have been found between (i) different identities in DID patients and (ii) perfusion before versus perfusion during "switching" between identities in a DID patient'.[5] This means that brain scans have shown different patterns of brain activity between different alters and during switching.

Specific parts of the brain have been shown to be different between people with and without DID. The limbic system is a collection of brain structures including the amygdala and the hippocampus. The limbic system is involved in processing memory and emotion and is affected by childhood trauma. An article called 'Dissociative Identity Disorder: A Pathophysiological Phenomenon' lists

MRI (magnetic resonance imaging) studies which show 'the limbic system of DID patients decreases in size (especially hippocampus and amygdala)'. It states 'the patients suffering with DID have been found to have some alterations in their brain morphology'.[6]

A more recent study called 'Aiding the diagnosis of dissociative identity disorder: A pattern recognition study of brain biomarkers'[7] also found differences between the DID brain and the brain of people without DID. King's College London commented on their study, saying that using MRI brain scans 'computers can "spot the difference" between healthy brains and the brains of people with Dissociative Identity Disorder'[8] on the basis of their brain structure. Reinders and Veltman reflect on the findings from their study in the article 'Dissociative identity disorder: Out of the shadows at last?',[9] where they outline the potential of future brain scans, stating 'structural brain imaging holds the promise of using objective biomarkers...to facilitate a fast and correct diagnosis of individuals with DID'. Scientific studies on DID are an important step towards DID and OSDD being taken more seriously by medical and mental health professionals. Reinders and Veltman recognise this and write that 'moving DID out of the shadows of psychiatry will facilitate earlier accurate diagnosis, faster and more targeted interventions, prevent unnecessary direct and indirect societal costs, but most important of all prevent years of suffering for individuals with the disorder'. Further research is needed on DID and the brain; however, preliminary evidence suggests that future studies may continue to reveal more and further help the DID and OSDD community. The article 'Treatment of dissociative identity disorder: Leveraging neurobiology to optimize success' states that 'prioritizing the voices of those with lived experience in the development, implementation, and interpretation of research is essential in optimizing treatment outcomes'.[10]

Fewer scientific studies have specifically focused on OSDD. Some older studies may refer to OSDD as DDNOS and some studies on dissociative disorders are applicable. Regarding OSDD and the brain, the findings are likely to be similar to the DID studies.

The areas which may be less similar are studies focusing on amnesia, which is not present with OSDD-1b, and studies looking at switching in OSDD-1a, where differences in brain imaging may be less pronounced. Further research is needed when it comes to OSDD and the brain. It must be noted that the brain can also recover from trauma through multiple biological, psychological and social processes, such as therapy.

Attachment Theory

+ **Attachment theory** was developed beginning in the late 1940s and 1950s by John Bowlby and later expanded by Mary Ainsworth.[11] It explains how the bond a child forms with their primary caregiver(s) can affect them.

+ **Attachment style** describes the way we connect with other people. Attachment styles are patterns of expectations and behaviours people develop about relationships with others, based on the relationship they had with their primary caregiver(s) as a child.

+ **Secure attachment** develops when the child's needs are met as an infant by their caregiver(s) in a nurturing environment, where they feel comforted and develop a sense of security.

+ **Insecure attachment** develops when the child's needs are not fully met as an infant by their caregiver(s), in an environment that may not have been nurturing. They may have not received comfort or felt safe. There are three insecure attachment styles: ambivalent, avoidant and disorganised.

People with DID and OSDD are more likely to have an insecure disorganised attachment style (also known as fearful-avoidant). Different alters in one system may also have different attachement styles. However, they can learn how to cope with and work through their attachment difficulties, such as through the relationship they have with a therapist. You can get an idea of your attachment style through a questionnaire provided by a mental health professional, or alternatively, through an online quiz, which may give a rough indication, but they are not diagnostic tools.

Multiplicity as a Spectrum

The Internal Family Systems (IFS) approach and many professionals trained in DID and OSDD believe that everyone has different parts, is multiple to some degree and that multiplicity exists on a broad spectrum. Some systems may find it comforting to know that others may also experience different parts. However, some systems may not like this idea because their parts do not manifest in the same way. DID and OSDD are at the far end of the multiplicity spectrum.

An example of multiplicity in those who do not have DID or OSDD would be people having their 'work self' and 'home self'. They may behave differently depending on the situation or environment. Some believe that people have different selves depending on what role they inhabit, such as a parent, lover or friend, while others view these simply as roles. Another example of this is the concept of an inner child.

However, the idea of multiplicity as a spectrum does not mean that non-systems have the same experience as people with DID or OSDD, nor does it mean that non-systems have alters or dissociated states of consciousness. Non-systems may have parts within one consciousness that are not fully developed, whereas in systems the personality never integrated to become one at a young age due to trauma and alters are fully formed. Multiplicity within non-systems is not the same as multiplicity within DID and OSDD and non-systems cannot claim to have the same experiences. DID and OSDD systems struggle with the manifestations of trauma and having different alters, whereas non-systems do not.

CHAPTER 4

DID and OSDD Fundamentals

The Different Types of Trauma

All DID and OSDD systems have experienced some form of child-hood trauma. Trauma usually occurs in early childhood. The book *Dissociative Identity Disorder: Treatment and Management* states that 'trauma must occur within an identified "developmental window", which generally occurs from ages 2 to 8'.[1] It also states that DID studies have shown that in most cases childhood trauma happens before the age of six.[2] Not all DID or OSDD systems were sexually abused.

Traumas that can cause DID or OSDD include (but are not limited to):

+ emotional/psychological abuse
+ physical abuse
+ sexual abuse
+ domestic violence
+ gang violence
+ abandonment
+ medical trauma, surgery or serious physical illness
+ human trafficking
+ war trauma
+ witnessing death
+ neglect

- bullying
- deprivation
- natural disaster
- (organised) ritual abuse
- generational trauma
- religious/spiritual abuse
- road accident
- any other traumatic event, e.g. losing a parent or caregiver.

Professionals generally believe that people with DID and OSDD have repeated, long-term or multiple traumas. However, other factors can also increase the likelihood of someone developing DID or OSDD, such as having multiple adverse childhood experiences (ACEs), being more prone to dissociation, having insecure attachment to caregivers, having a lower window of tolerance, a family history of trauma, a child coping with their trauma alone, a child having a very imaginative or sensitive personality and being neurodiverse.

Many traumatised children do not tell anyone their trauma because they are told to keep it a secret by abusers and they may be threatened with horrible consequences. Other times, children may not know that what is happening is actually wrong or bad because they are too young to understand, or they do not yet have the vocabulary to describe what is actually happening.

TIPS FOR SUPPORTING PEOPLE WITH DID AND OSDD
Remember that it is not your right to know about someone else's trauma, so be mindful when asking about it. Do not expect a system to tell you their trauma and never pressure them to speak about it. Trauma can be a difficult, heavy, delicate, complex and triggering topic for people with DID and OSDD. If you are a loved one or therapist, they might not mind telling you about it, although everyone is different. If they do disclose any information about their trauma, it

should be kept confidential. Do not tell anyone else externally and do not tell any other alters in their system. This is because some alters may not be aware of what the system's trauma is.

Trauma as a Child

It is important for the information in this book to be put into context. The only reason DID and OSDD exist is because of trauma. The reality is children have been hurt, are still being hurt today and will continue to be hurt in the future. This is not ok. We need to be aware of this when speaking about multiplicity. Within all systems is a hurt child or hurt children.

System Sizes

System size refers to how many alters exist within a DID or OSDD system. The diagnostic criteria state that a system must have at least two alters. Yet system sizes can vary greatly. Some systems may be small, with just a few alters. Some systems may have a dozen alters, some several dozens. Some systems may be large and have around 100 alters, while some have may have hundreds. The book *Dissociative Identity Disorder: Treatment and Management* states 'alter personalities can vary in number from one to thousands' and that 'the average number of personalities in someone with DID is 13–15'.[3] All systems are valid regardless of how many alters they have.

> ## OUR EXPERIENCE
> *When we first realised that we had DID, we were aware of several alters in our system. Over time, we discovered more. Once we started therapy specifically for our DID, the number of alters we met increased further. We currently have around 100 alters in our system. Each of us are unique and have our own interests, likes,*

dislikes, opinions and desires, just like any other human. We used to feel ashamed of having this many alters, but now we see it as a sign of healing. In order for us to heal, we must meet everyone in our system. Despite having many alters, it is usually just a handful who take turns fronting.

Alters
Types of Alters

Alter type helps to categorise different alters. Not every system will have all the different alter types listed and some systems may not use these terms. Some alters may also age slide, meaning that they can age up or down. The most common alter types are outlined below, although some systems may also have other types not listed here.

- **Adult alters** can be young adults, midlife adults and older adults. For example, some systems may have grandparent alters. Adult alters tend to manage everyday life, go to work, deal with responsibilities, stay organised and help the system to function. Adult alters can form when the body is both a child and an adult. They can form during childhood as a way to help cope with and give a greater sense of protection from trauma. Adult alters can be trauma holders if the system experiences trauma as an adult.

- **ANP** stands for apparently normal part. ANPs are part of the theory of structural dissociation. The more modern term used is the 'Going On With Normal Life' part.[4] ANPs may not know about the system's trauma, which allows them to get on with everyday life.

- **Autopilot alters** are alters who take care of the basic and essential life tasks when no one else can, such as keeping up hygiene and eating. Another name for this alter may be 'operator'. In neuroscience this is called the default mode network.

+ **Baby or infant alters** are alters who are of this age. Some systems may have had trauma as an infant or baby, which means that they may have alters from this stage in their life. Baby/ infant alters may not know how to talk, walk or understand things. They may think and behave the same way that real babies do. However, some baby/infant alters may be able to talk/walk/understand because they belong to a system of alters who are capable of those skils. Some baby/infant alters may also be trauma holders. Baby/infant alters should always be protected and taken care of.

+ **Core** is *said* to be the 'first' alter to have existed, or the 'original' identity before alters developed. The theory of structural dissociation does not support the idea of the core and it is not part of any diagnostic criteria. The concept of a core is based on older theories and is not endorsed by many mental health professionals or systems. Instead, all alters are regarded as equal.

+ **Dead alters** are alters who appear dead. Alters cannot die but it can feel like they have died or ceased to exist. Examples of 'dead' alters include angels, ghosts, zombies and skeletons. Alters may 'die' in response to overwhelming trauma and some alters may appear dead in the inner world, for example by not moving.

+ **Dormant alters** are like dormant volcanoes and can be thought of as 'sleeping'. They still exist but may not have fronted or been conscious in some time. Dormant alters may be dormant for months, years or decades. Dormant alters can be hidden away from the rest of the system and may be in a different location to the other alters in the inner world.

- **EP** stands for emotional part. EPs are part of the theory of structural dissociation. EPs hold the trauma. They can also display a range of behaviour such as fight, flight and freeze.

- **Factives** are alters based on a real-life person, such as a famous person, a person from history or someone that the system looks up to, like a kind teacher or friend. Factives may be created because the system finds a person's characteristics helpful, like someone who is strong, confident or comforting. Factives may look like the real-life person in the inner world and feel like them too. They can also have their own individual experiences and personalities. Sometimes, persecutors may be factives of abusers or someone connected to the system's trauma. Factives are a type of introject.

- **Fictives** are alters based on fictional characters, such as characters from a book, film or television show. Fictives may be created because the system finds a person's characteristics helpful, like someone who is calm, heroic or outgoing. They may look like the fictional character in the inner world and feel like them too. Fictives can have memories from their source material. They can also have their own individual experiences and personalities. Fictives are a type of introject.

- **Fragments** are alters that are not fully developed. They may not have a fully formed personality and hold just one emotion, memory or purpose. Several fragments may hold different memories of the same trauma. Some people with OSDD may have more fragments than alters.[5]

- **Introjects** are alters who are based on external people, characters or concepts. They may form around someone's identity, personality traits or (perceived) presence. Introjects can be split into two categories: factives (based on real people) and fictives (based on fictional characters). Like other alters, introjects can take on a variety of roles within the system and be more than one alter type, such as protectors, persecutors or non-human alters.

+ **Littles** are alters who are the age of a child. They are also called child alters and often speak, think and act like real children, even in covert systems. Some littles are trauma holders, and some are not. All systems will have or have had at least one little who is a trauma holder. Some littles may have memories of being present when the body was a child. Littles should always be protected and taken care of.

+ **Manic alters** are alters that experience mania. When they are close to the front or fronting, the whole system may feel more manic, such as with more energy, hyperawareness, racing thoughts and heightened senses. Experiencing mania can be scary for systems as they may feel out of control. Manic alters may engage in risky behaviours due to their mania.

+ **Middles** are preteen alters aged 8–12. Some systems use the term middles, while other systems just use the terms littles and teen alters.

+ **Non-human alters** are alters who are not human. Some examples include animals, fantasy creatures like fairies, demons, vampires, robots and objects such as a tree or rock. Non-human alters may find it challenging or disorienting to front in the real world, especially when a system's body looks very different to their inner world, like a fairy alter who has wings in the inner world.

+ **Non-speaking alters** are alters who are mute, who do not speak or who cannot speak. Some infant/baby alters may be non-speaking. It is important to provide these alters with the space and methods to communicate if they would like to. Do not force them to speak. Instead, they could try communicating through writing, journalling, drawing, art making, through play such as with toys or through movement like dancing or acting. Somatic alters can also be non-speaking. Alternative therapies may be helpful for non-speaking alters.

+ **NPC** stands for non-playable character. NPCs are people/beings who live in the inner world as background characters, but they are not alters. An example would be a gardener who tends to a garden in the inner world.

+ **Opposite sex/gender alters** are alters who have a different gender than what the body was assigned at birth. In one system there can be alters of many different genders.

+ **Persecutors** are alters who may act in a harmful way to the system such as self-harming the body. Even if it does not appear so, persecutors may be trying to help protect the system. Persecutors may sometimes be introjects of abusers. Some systems will tell their abuser introjects to leave their system, believing they were never meant to be part of it. Persecutors are not 'evil alters'. Systems do not have 'evil alters'.

+ **Self** is a term used in the Internal Family Systems (IFS) model of psychotherapy. It is the idea that everyone has a core 'Self' (energy) as well as other parts.

+ **Sexual alters** are alters who may front during physically intimate relationships to help protect other alters from experiencing something that could be triggering. Sexual alters may have specifically been created to handle sexual trauma, sexual experiences or to prevent other alters from knowing about it. Some sexual alters also hold memories of sexual trauma which cannot be accessed by other alters. Some sexual alters are hypersexual.

+ **Sibling alters** are alters who may be related to each other or feel like they are related to each other. For example, alters who are brothers, sisters, siblings, twins or triplets. Systems may also have other familial or familial-like relationships between alters.

+ **Somatic alters** are alters that live in a certain part of the body and/or may communicate somatically (using the body) such as by causing pain.

+ **Suicidal alters** are alters who have suicidal ideations and may make plans to end the body's life. Some suicidal alters may have attempted suicide before. Some suicidal alters may be trauma holders and/or a child or teen alter.

+ **Teen alters** are alters who are the age of a teenager. They are likely to have been created when the body was a teenager, although this is not always the case. They may have memories from when the body was a teenager.

People with DID and OSDD can also have alters who experience additional mental health symptoms or have other mental health diagnoses. For example, a system may have an alter who experiences delusions or an alter who has OCD.

Alter Roles
Alter type and alter role are different. Alter role describes the 'job' that a particular alter has or the reason why they were created. Alters do not usually choose their roles. Some may not have a specific role while others may have more than one. Not all systems will have alters who fulfill all of the different roles. The most common alter

roles are outlined below, though some systems may have additional roles not listed here.

- **Caretakers** are protectors who take care of and look after other alters within their system. They may also look after other people outside of their system. Caretakers can be maternal and often look after littles.

- **Function holders** are alters who take control of particular tasks, such as cleaning, cooking or managing life admin.

- **Gatekeepers** are alters who control switching, access to the front, access to the inside, access to other alters and access to certain memories, such as trauma memories. Some systems may also have dissociative alters who prevent memory access but who are not fully formed alters.

- **Host** is the alter who most commonly uses the body, who is present more often or fronts more than the other alters. Some systems have more than one host and not all systems will have a host. Having no host may make navigating every-day life more difficult. Some systems have a rotating host, where different alters take turns as host. Other systems may have a co-host who shares the role of host.

- **Internal self helpers** are logical and knowledgeable alters who understand the system and the other alters, how it functions and may also know about the trauma. They help the system internally.

- **Managers/organisers** are practical alters who help with planning, organisation and delegating tasks. Some systems may refer to their managers as internal self helpers, while others may differentiate them.

+ **Memory holders** are alters who hold specific memories. They will usually hold traumatic memories, but some memory holders also hold happy memories that are not related to trauma. These alters can also be littles.

+ **Mood/emotion holders** are alters who hold or express a particular emotion, such as sadness, anger or shame. Some emotion holders may be fragments and/or trauma holders.

+ **Protectors** are alters who protect the body and the system. While protectors are often adults, they can also be teen or child alters. Some alters may not seem like protectors, such as suicidal alters; however, they are protectors if their intent is to protect the system.

+ **Social alters** are alters who tend to front during social situations. They may be more extroverted and enjoy socialising more than other alters.

+ **Soothers** are alters who help to soothe and calm down other alters internally or externally.

+ **Trauma holders** are alters who hold memories of trauma. One system may have experienced multiple traumas, meaning different alters may hold the different memories of each trauma. Additionally, there can be multiple alters who hold different *types* of memories from the *same* trauma, such as the emotional, physical, factual or visual memories.

People with OSDD-1 who have less distinct alters may not have different types of alters or alters with different roles.

TIPS FOR SUPPORTING PEOPLE WITH DID AND OSDD

- Treat alters like you would any other person and as separate individuals.
- Remember that not all alters will have the same interests, opinions or boundaries.
- Avoid picking favourite alters.
- If you know or have been asked to, try to use the right alter name. If you are unsure, just ask.
- Remember that not all systems will have a host. If a system has a host, do not treat them like the 'real' alter or refer to other alters as if they belong to the host.
- Not everyone in a system may know or remember you, so be sure to check and introduce yourself if needed.
- The system's outer appearance and voice may change depending on who is fronting; try not to make a big deal out of this and avoid making negative comments about it.
- Remember, systems do not have evil alters.

OUR EXPERIENCE

When we first met newly discovered alters in our system it was overwhelming and we thought it meant that we were becoming more unwell. However, we now know that learning more about our system is imperative to our recovery journey. It is also important for all alters in a system to feel welcomed, seen and heard. After all, some of them have been hidden since early childhood. Additionally, over time, we have learned that the 'difficult' alters in our system, such as the suicidal, angry and doubtful-of-our-DID alters, are all actually protectors. This has been a revelation. We truly are all in this together and we are so grateful for all our alters. At times we still meet newly discovered alters and very occasionally new alters may be created in times of extreme stress.

Hearing Voices?

Some people assume that DID and OSDD systems can hear voices. This is not necessarily the case. Some systems may hear the voices of their alters inside their head. Other systems may just hear one internal monologue and others may be able to distinguish their thoughts as other alters' thoughts. All systems are valid regardless of whether they can hear their alters or not. However, the important factor here is that the 'voices' are heard *inside* the head rather than *outside*. Hearing voices outside of the head can be a symptom of a separate condition, such as schizophrenia, which is not a dissociative disorder. Systems who can hear other alters are **not** having auditory hallucinations. Some systems may also have schizophrenia, but this is a small minority. Confusion about how people define 'hearing voices' can mean that some systems are misdiagnosed with schizophrenia.

PART 2

Living with DID and OSDD

CHAPTER 5

All About Switching and Fronting

Fronting

Fronting refers to the alter who is currently present and in control of the body. The alter fronting is the alter 'in the front'. In systems, different alters take turns fronting. An example is 'I, Sage, am an alter in this system. I am currently fronting. The last time I fronted was a few weeks ago. I like being in the front.' Systems can also experience co-fronting. This is when two or more alters front at the same time.

TIPS FOR SUPPORTING PEOPLE WITH DID AND OSDD

- Try not to assume you know who is fronting and remember that different alters may remember different things.
- If you know them, you may want to ask the system 'May I ask who is fronting right now?' However, respect that some systems may not feel comfortable telling you, may not feel comfortable being open about their system, or may not wish to bother introducing everyone to all their alters.
- You then may want to ask 'Have we met before?' If they respond no, introduce yourself and explain your

---

> relationship to them, e.g. 'I am Hunter, a friend of the system, it's lovely to meet you!'
> - Remember that it is not essential for you to know who is fronting, especially if the system does not feel comfortable telling you.

Frontstuck

Frontstuck refers to a situation where the alter who is fronting has been fronting for a long time and feels like they are stuck, because other alters have not switched with them. Being frontstuck may be nice for the alter who is fronting if they do not mind being in the front. However, for some alters they may not like being frontstuck for a variety of reasons, such as feeling very tired after fronting for a long time. It can also potentially be dangerous and scary if a little gets frontstuck by themselves as this could make the system more vulnerable. To stop being frontstuck a system could try asking inside for someone else to front, such as by speaking directly to other alters and using their name. Alternatively, they could try to positively trigger out another alter that they know would not mind fronting, such as by listening to their favourite podcast.

Switching

A switch is when one alter who is in control of the body changes/ switches place with another alter. An example is Alter A is fronting, Alter B switches with Alter A, resulting in Alter B now being the one in the front. Alter A may have been sent back into the inner world, or could also remain fronting with Alter B; this is called co-fronting or co-consciousness.

What Does Switching Feel and Look Like?

Switches can feel and look different for different systems and different alters.

How Switching Feels

+ Switches can make systems feel:
  - confused
  - spacey or faint
  - dissociated
  - surprised if the switch was unexpected.
+ The alter fronting can feel like they are being pulled back-
  wards or pulled underwater.
+ The alter fronting may be waiting for the switch to happen.
+ Switching can give some systems/alters headaches.
+ Switching can feel unpleasant.
+ For the alter fronting they start to lose consciousness, which
  feels similar to losing consciousness before you fall asleep.

How Switching Looks

+ Switches can look like:
  - the system stopping what they are doing and becoming
    still
  - the system looking tired or confused
  - the system staring into space
  - the system blinking a lot
  - the system closing their eyes or looking down
  - a physical jolt or small head movement.
+ Sometimes a switch does not happen easily or quickly.
+ Switches can be very subtle. Others may not be able to spot
  a switch happening and sometimes there may be no signs
  of one happening at all.

How Long Do Switches Take?

Switches usually do not take that long to happen. They usually take
several seconds or minutes. However, sometimes switches can be
slow, taking a couple of hours, days or more. This may happen for a
reason, such as someone trying to prevent a switch from happening.

Systems can feel 'switchy', before a switch happens, which can be a sign they may switch. Feeling 'switchy' can be described as feeling dissociated, having an awareness of other alters around and noticing a change in internal dynamics. Systems will usually feel switchy for several seconds or minutes and may sometimes feel switchy for hours or days.

How Often Do Switches Happen?

This varies between systems. Different systems will switch different amounts. Systems may switch dozens of times a day, several times a day, once a day, every few days, a couple times a week, every few weeks, every few months or more. The frequency of switching can also change over time or be irregular.

Can Alters Switch Whenever They Want?

This depends on the system and the alters. Some are able to switch when they want, some can sometimes and others are unable to. It may feel frustrating not being able to switch in or out if you would like to. Some systems use positive triggers to help an alter switch, such as playing an alter's favourite song, which can bring them closer to the front. Over time, through recovery, therapy and gaining greater system communication, alters may be more able to control their switches.

How and Why Do Alters Switch?

Switches can be consensually agreed upon, positively or negatively triggered, or forced. A positive trigger is when something positive gains the attention of a particular alter(s), such as littles seeing a soft toy. A negative trigger is a negative reminder, such as seeing something that is a reminder of a trauma. Systems can be triggered by any of the five senses. Some switches may be planned, such as making sure a particular alter is fronting for a medical appointment. Other switches are agreed upon in the moment by the alters involved. A forced switch could be done with good or bad intentions. Systems with less communication may sometimes have to just do what they think is in the system's best interests. The cause of the switch may not always be known to the system.

Who Switches?

Who switches will depend on the trigger or who a system decides should switch. Some systems have a gatekeeper alter(s) who can control who switches when. They may be the only alter who has control over switches. Some alters may switch less than others. Some traumaversaries, anniversaries of trauma, may cause a particular alter(s) to front. Systems try to make sure that littles only switch when it is safe for them to do so.

Can You Tell When Someone Is Switching?

Often switches are not obvious and you would not be able to tell if a switch is happening. People who know what to look for may be able to guess when a switch is happening. Some switches may be more obvious than others and some systems may have more obvious switches than others.

Can a System Stop a Switch?

Yes, some systems and alters may try to prevent a switch from happening and this can sometimes work. There are many reasons why an alter may want to prevent a switch, such as they want to stay fronting, they are afraid that the alter who is close could harm the system if they front or a little was triggered and is trying to front but the system does not feel that it is safe for them to front.

Will an Alter Remember What Was Happening Before They Switched?

This depends on the system and the alters. Some systems have full amnesia between different alters, meaning they will not know what was just happening. Some systems have partial amnesia so may have a vague idea what was going on. Other systems may know what was going on. OSDD-1b systems have less amnesia between alters, so are more likely to remember what was happening before, during and after a switch. Over time, through recovery, the amnesia between different alters can lessen.

OSDD and Switching

For people with OSDD-1a (who have less distinct alters) and for people with partial DID, they generally switch a lot less frequently compared to someone with DID. This is usually because they have a host who fronts most of the time. For people with OSDD-1b (who have distinct alters but no amnesia) they usually switch more frequently than those with OSDD-1a. They may also find switching easier, due to having no amnesia between their alters and therefore greater system communication.

TIPS FOR SUPPORTING PEOPLE WITH DID AND OSDD

- A switch may happen without you noticing.
- Do not ask, encourage, trigger or force a system to switch unless you have been asked to do so.
- Try not to make a scene when a switch happens.
- Give a system time and space if they are switching.
- If applicable, let them know who you are, where you are and what you are doing if they switch.

Rapid Switching

Rapid switching is when many switches happen in quick succession in a short period of time. Rapid switching can be confusing, disorientating, exhausting and may cause other symptoms such as headaches. Some systems report that consuming alcohol or recreational drugs can make rapid switching more likely. However, this is not the case for all systems.

Logging Switches

It can be beneficial to log your system's switches as it can teach you more about your system's patterns and triggers. This could be done in your system journal (see Chapter 9), your phone or anywhere else you will all remember. You can reserve a few pages in the back of your journal for this or create separate switching logs. Having these headings can be helpful:

Date/Time of Day	Who Switched?	Why Did You Switch? (What Was the Trigger?)

OUR EXPERIENCE

Our system's switches are usually every few weeks, but it can vary. Sometimes it can be less and sometimes it can be more. We can also feel when other alters are closer to the front. To us, switching can feel disorienting. We feel spacey and start blinking lots, our eyes then close and when we open them someone else may have switched. We are also more likely to switch in therapy as this time is dedicated to our DID.

Co-Consciousness and Passive Influence

+ **Co-consciousness** is when more than one alter is present at the same time. It is sometimes abbreviated to 'co-con'.

+ **Co-fronting** is when more than one alter is fronting at the same time.

+ **Passive influence** is when other alters subtly influence the alter who is fronting. For example, an alter who is not fronting may get triggered by something and feel sad. The alter fronting may also feel this sadness, even though it is not theirs. Another example is an adult alter fronting in a grocery store who felt a strong urge to buy a toy; this urge was actually passive influence from a child alter. Passive influence is more subtle than blending. With passive influence the alter fronting still mostly feels like themselves.

+ **Blending** is when another alter is so close to the front that their emotions, thoughts or behaviours feel like your own. It might not be obvious that what you are feeling belongs to another alter. Recognising that some of the emotions you feel when fronting may not be your own can be an important step in recovery.

+ **The car analogy** is used to describe multiplicity. The car represents the body and the person driving represents the alter who is currently fronting and in control of the body. The passenger in the front seat next to the driver represents co-consciousness, as they can see out of the car's front window/the body's eyes, but they are not in control of the body/car. The passengers in the back of the car represent all the other alters in the system. They can influence the alters in the front; this is passive influence. A car that has two steering wheels allowing two people to be in control of the car represents co-fronting, where more than one alter is in control of the body at the same time.

What Does Co-Consciousness Feel Like?

Co-consciousness is like:

+ piggyback riding
+ sharing a tandem bicycle
+ a mental tug of war
+ partial body autonomy

+ having a roommate
+ a more extreme version of feeling two emotions at once
+ someone looking over your shoulder and through your eyes.

Co-conscious Littles

Adult alters can be co-conscious with littles. This can feel strange, a child and adult sharing one body consciously and at the same time. There are some nice aspects and difficulties of being co-conscious with a little. Overall, it can be a healing experience. Littles are able to be a child again but remain safer as an adult alter is also around.

Feeling Blurry/Blended (Not Knowing Who Is Fronting)

Blended refers to when two or more alters are mixed together, so they do not feel like their fully separate selves. Instead, they may feel like a single, combined experience or presence. Blending is different from co-consciousness, where there is a dual (or multiple) awareness of separate identities at the same time.

Sometimes systems do not know who is fronting. This is sometimes referred to as feeling blurry or blended. This can happen when multiple alters are fronting at the same and it is not clear who is in control. Other times, it may feel like no one is fully fronting or that several alters are around or near the front. Feeling blurry or blended or not having anyone entirely in the front can feel confusing. Systems may prefer to know who is fronting. Feeling blurry may last anywhere from a few minutes to a few days, weeks or more. Sometimes when systems feel blurry, they may try to positively trigger a particular alter so that they can fully front. An example of this would be to spray the alter's favourite perfume, read their favourite book or wear their favourite clothing. Feeling blurry or blended is also sometimes described as feeling 'switchy', like a switch is about to happen.

When systems start to recover they may find that they become more blended and it becomes harder to decipher who is fronting.

This blending may feel more natural. This blending occurs as the amnesic walls between alters begin to break down through trauma work.

CHAPTER 6

Understanding Alters

For OSDD-1a systems who have less distinct alters, some of the following information may be less applicable. OSDD-1a systems are just as valid as OSDD-1b and DID systems.

All About Littles

Littles are child alters. The age range that defines a little can vary from person to person. Some may consider littles to be aged 8 and under, aged 10 and under, aged 12 and under or aged 18 and under. Some people also refer to alters aged 13–18 as teen alters, alters aged 8–12 as middles and alters aged 3 and under as baby or infant alters.

Littles are not the same as non-system's 'inner child'. Littles are fully developed alters, most of whom were formed during childhood. Just like adult alters, littles can have different names, ages, likes, dislikes, fears, interests and ways of presenting. They may also hold memories of when they fronted as a child.

Littles usually think, speak and act the same way a regular child does. Littles may have a childlike voice that is different to the voices of adult alters and it may be higher in pitch. Even in covert systems, if a little fronts, their presentation may be more overt and obvious. Being a child in an adult body may be difficult. It may feel scary and confusing. Some littles may also be non-speaking. This could be because they are too young to know how to speak, which may be the case for some baby or infant alters, or because of trauma. Some littles may be more knowledgeable about certain topics than a real child and may understand more complex matters. This is because they belong to a system that also has older alters. Like real children, littles may have less energy than a teen or adult and may become overwhelmed or exhausted more easily.

Littles are the most vulnerable alters in a system. They should be looked after and taken great care of. For some systems, littles may not act like children or may not want to be treated like one. All systems are different and can therefore vary; if you are unsure, you can ask them.

Do All People with DID and OSDD Have Littles?

Everyone with DID and OSDD will have once had at least one little. This is because these conditions are formed in childhood. Most systems still have littles but some systems may no longer have any littles due to the fusion and integration of alters in therapy.

Are All Littles Trauma Holders?

No, not all littles are trauma holders. A trauma holding little is a child alter who experienced childhood trauma. There can be multiple littles who hold different parts of the same trauma and there can also be multiple littles who hold different traumas. Being a trauma holder does not necessarily mean the little knows all the details of that trauma; for example, they may only hold the emotional sensory memories.

How Many Littles Do People with DID and OSDD Have?

This depends on each system. Some may have just one little, others may have several, a dozen or a larger number of littles. People with a larger system will likely have more littles. Some people assume that the more littles a system has, the more difficulties or trauma they may have experienced as a child, because alters are always created for a reason. However, having only a few littles does not mean someone's trauma is any less valid or severe.

76

Littles Fronting

Systems may feel embarrassed if a little fronts but they should not let this get in the way of helping their littles. Littles who have not fronted after many years and sometimes decades may not recognise their surroundings, such as if the current home is not the one they grew up in as a child. For some littles, fronting may feel scary or overwhelming.

Keeping littles safe when they front is very important. The adult alters in the system should do all they can to help a little if they front. The first thing to check is where your system is. If you are outside in public or at work or school, then an adult alter should immediately try to switch with the little. This is because it may not be safe for them, they may be scared or not understand where they are, they may not realise that they are more vulnerable or they may not understand the role the system is currently in, e.g. their work role. You can tell the little 'Hello (little's name) it is (adult alter's name). I am afraid it is not the best time for you to front right now but we will make sure you can front again soon (insert when, like when we get home or in our next therapy session).' If you are at home or in therapy, then your system can decide if it is safe or the right moment for the little to front.

As a little it may feel confusing to front and scary to experience flashbacks. Here are some ideas on how to help:

+ Hug a soft toy or blanket.
+ Eat your favourite food/drink/snack.
+ Do some drawing, colouring-in or use stickers.
+ Watch your favourite TV show or film.
+ Read a picture book.
+ Put on some cosy clothes or your favourite clothes (like a fluffy jumper).
+ Ask inside if an adult alter could front/switch/be co-conscious.
+ If things all feel too much you could have a nap or go to bed early.

- If you have a therapist or know someone who understands your littles, you could message or call them.

Some people with DID and OSDD may feel apprehensive about allowing littles to front, but allowing them to front in the right circumstances can be positive, healing and important.

Positives of Littles Fronting

- Seeing the world from a child's perspective again can be magical and something only systems are truly able to ever experience again.
- You can really enjoy the little things, such as getting excited about activities like going on a train journey or doing some colouring.
- It is nice for littles to front after so long and for them to enjoy life as a child.
- It is healing for trauma holding littles to see that there is more to life than having trauma.
- Littles can feel comforted by nostalgic films, children's TV shows or toys.
- It can be an important step in a system's recovery journey for the littles to front, for them to be seen and heard by the adult alters after being 'hidden' for so long.
- It can give you a reason to live. Staying alive for the sake of the littles, who deserve to live and be protected.

Difficulties of Littles Fronting

- Completing adult tasks like working and paying the rent and bills can be impossible or very hard, overwhelming and confusing.
- It may feel sad that the little wants to play outside with other children but cannot do this as they are in an adult's body.

- A little may not know the system's partner or friends or be scared of them as they are adults.
- It can be hard to act like an adult when you feel like a child.
- Doing even a simple task like making food may become a bigger, more difficult task.

Littles and Recovery

For a system to recover, the littles need to be helped in therapy. They do not necessarily have to front, but they must be able to at least communicate through another alter in their system. It is especially important that littles who hold trauma are unburdened from their trauma through therapy. Unburdening littles allows them to live like a child again and experience a safe and happy life. When littles are brought into the present, they realise that they are no longer stuck in the past and they can see that the system is safe now. If a little wants to front in therapy you should let them; just make sure a responsible adult alter fronts before you finish your session, to help keep everyone safe afterwards. Once littles are helped in therapy they may age up to become older or want to fuse with other alters, like adult alters. This may feel sad for some alters but it is a sign of healing. Fusions can still occur in systems whose recovery goal is functional multiplicity.

Looking After Littles

In addition to therapy, there are also other ways to help look after littles. These can include:

- communicating with them and letting them express how they feel (e.g. through an internal conversation, therapeutic art or journalling)
- validating their feelings and reminding them they are safe now
- comforting them
- allowing them to front when it is safe

- gently asking them to stay in the inner world if something outside could be triggering.

Some littles enjoy playing with toys, watching children's television shows or films, listening to music or playing games. Many systems find it helpful to have specific items just for littles, for example, a special box that might include soft toys (stuffies), colouring books, sticker or activity books, children's picture books, other toys, clothes they like, a soft blanket or anything else that brings them joy or comfort.

In some systems, protector and caretaker alters help look after littles, while in others adult alters take on these roles. Particular alters may also care for littles in the inner world.

Littles should always be treated as one would treat a real child: with kindness, patience and respect for their developmental stage. It's important to speak about age-appropriate topics and avoid anything 'adult' that could be upsetting or triggering, such as swearing or discussing traumatic events.

Littles may need more support than adult alters and may not be able to handle everyday tasks on their own. For example, they may struggle to find their way home, cook, write emails, clean or go to work or school. To keep littles safe, systems should avoid sharing information about them online. However, it can be helpful to share information with trusted people in real life, if the system feels comfortable doing so.

Having a plan of what to do if a little fronts can also be helpful. Some systems like to carry a DID or OSDD emergency/crisis/ medical card around with them. Similar to someone who carries around a medical identity card for a physical health condition, the DID/OSDD card can be shown to others when in need. Such as if a little fronts in public or if you have a mental health crisis. The cards explain what these conditions are and have space to add an emergency contact. People like to keep them in their wallet, purse, bag, car or lanyard.

It could be helpful to have a note that your system keeps to show littles when they front for the first time. The note could say something like:

Hello, nice to meet you! This is a note to say that you belong to a system of others. This means you share your body with other people...

Add any information you think would be helpful. You may also wish to write the note in big clear handwriting and add some colour or drawings.

TIPS FOR SUPPORTING PEOPLE WITH DID AND OSDD

- Talk to littles how you would talk to a real child, make sure you are age appropriate and look out for them.
- Be careful what you speak to littles about, such as avoiding adult subjects, Father Christmas etc.

New and Dormant Alters

New alters can develop as a coping mechanism at any point in a system's life following trauma. This includes in childhood, in adolescence and in adulthood. New alters can be created after additional trauma or for other reasons which would help the system, such as the creation of an alter to help keep up with schoolwork. It is important for new alters to be warmly welcomed into their system.

As well as new alters being created, over time, systems may also find out about newly *discovered* alters. Newly discovered alters are alters that the system did not know existed, making them seem new even though they are not. Finding out about these alters may make a system feel like it is growing, but these alters were always there. Newly discovered alters may be newly aware, previously dormant or recently discovered by other alters.

It may be overwhelming to learn about new, newly discovered or dormant alters. Try to have an open mind and show everyone in your system kindness. It can also be overwhelming for new alters to find out that they are part of a system. Different alters may have varying levels of acceptance. It may be helpful to have a note to show a new alter to inform them about your system. You could include whether you have DID or OSDD and what this means, how many alters there are in your system, a list of alter names/ages/roles and a brief summary of what your days look like, such as going to work or volunteering. Different systems have varying levels of amnesia, so some new alters may already know about the system or be able to access more information inside.

Making Alter Profiles

Creating alter profiles is a helpful way to organise and keep track of information about each alter. This allows alters to learn more about each other and makes it easier to share information with your family, friends or therapist (if the system/alters agree to it). If you decide to include information about your trauma, you might want to put a (trigger) warning. Collating information about each alter can help systems in their recovery journey.

Some systems like to use images of other people as 'faceclaims' to represent what their alters look like in their inner world. It may also be helpful to create mood boards for each alter, documenting what they are like and what they like, such as objects, places, clothes, colours and hobbies.

Some people with DID and OSDD like to draw their alters or create alter self-portraits. Other systems may prefer to create digital avatars. These are fun things to do and may be useful but are not essential. Some systems may not know what their alters look like and that's ok.

Here are some suggestions of what you could include in your alter profiles:

Name:
Age:
Gender, Pronouns, Sexuality:
System Role/Alter Type: *(Are they a trauma holder? A protector?)*
Personality and Appearance:
Likes, Dislikes and Interests:
Where do you live in the inner world/body?
When were you created and why?
History:
Important information: *(Such as any special skills/harmful behaviours/ triggers)*
Relationships to other alters?
Notes: *(Such as have you been helped/unburdened in therapy?)*

Alter Names

Some alters may know their name, some you may need to ask and others may be unsure or not have a name. Naming your alters can be helpful. It makes talking about them and identifying them easier. Your alters can choose whichever name they like, within reason. It may be hard trying to choose a name. Some alters choose names they already like or base it off characters' names or people they know. Picking a name may seem overwhelming but try and think of it as fun. Some people with OSDD-1a may not have names for their alters as they are less distinct, and that's ok.

> **OUR EXPERIENCE**
> *If some of our alters do not already have a name or cannot immedi-*
> *ately think of one they like, we have found it helpful to do an online*
> *search of baby names and have a look through the lists. You can also*
> *be more specific with searching such as girls' names, boys' names,*
> *gender neutral names, short names, unusual names or names begin-*
> *ning with a specific letter.*

Different Interests

In one system different alters can have very different interests and skills to each other. One alter may love folk music, one may love rap and one may love jazz. Some alters may love creating art; others may not. Some may be great at writing poetry; others may be great at baking. Some may enjoy playing sports; others may prefer gaming, gardening or reading. Alters are distinct individuals, just like people who are not plural. For some people with DID and OSDD, muscle memory exists for some activities, such as everyone in the system being able to play the piano, drive a car or write. In OSDD-1a systems the alters may be less distinct.

Having varying interests in one system is similar to the 'renaissance man'. These varying interests may also exist in terms of alters' career desires. One alter may want to be a nurse, one an astronaut and one an artist. Having varied career desires can make deciding what career path to take or what to study at university more difficult. For systems that have hosts, they may decide to follow the host's career desires. Other systems may decide to have a group vote between the whole system or between those who front most often.

Can Alters Die?

Alters cannot die. However, it can *feel* like an alter has died. Some non-human alters may feel like they are dead, such as an angel or ghost alter. Alters may appear to have died if the system experienced a near death experience or a trauma that they felt they would not survive. Alters do not die when they fuse, split, integrate, go dormant or even with 'final' fusion.

Fusion and Splitting
Fusion

A fusion is when two or more alters join/fuse and come together to become one. A fusion results in the amnesic walls breaking down between the alters involved, and there can be an integration of memories. Some fusions happen subconsciously, without the system knowing, and some are consciously agreed upon. Fusions which come as a surprise may be harder to accept. Sometimes systems will grieve the separate alters that fused. Alters cannot die but it may feel this way. Over time, in therapy, fusions may become more frequent. They can be a sign of healing. Some child alters may wish to fuse with adult alters; this can be a healing experience. When a fusion is consciously agreed upon, it is likely that the need for it still arose naturally. When a fusion is a conscious decision, it is important that all alters involved consent to it happening. A fusion should never be forced. Fusions can also become undone between alters; this is known as a split.

OUR EXPERIENCE

The first fusion we experienced was during a stressful time in our life. It was sad because it was unexpected and we missed the two individual alters. However, we know it happened to help our system. We have since experienced beautiful fusions, which felt so right. We have also noticed that, over time, alters can change and evolve individually, in the same way that all humans can change over time.

Splitting

Splitting is the opposite of fusion. With a fusion, two or more alters merge together to become one. With a split, an alter divides to become two or more alters. Splitting can happen due to something difficult, stressful or traumatic going on in a system's present life. Systems can be aware or unaware of a split happening, but alters cannot force a split themselves. Instead, a split usually arises naturally. However, alters may be able to consent or refuse consent, thus stopping or allowing one to continue. Alters who are created from a split can have characteristics and personalities from the alter they split from. Splitting can be difficult for systems. Systems may get used to the alters who exist in their system, and changes to this can be hard to process. Systems may feel sad that they are splitting as it may seem like the opposite to recovery. Remember your system knows what is best for you and splitting happens for a reason, whether you are aware of it or not.

CHAPTER 7

All About Systems

This chapter covers all aspects of systems, from overt, covert and polyfragmented systems to their inner worlds.

Signs You May Be a System
Physical Signs

+ Seeing different handwriting styles in your writing, without having done it deliberately.
+ Being told by others that your appearance, personality or mannerisms drastically change sometimes.
+ Noticing changes in the sound of your voice, which were not done deliberately.
+ Finding notes or drawings that you have no memory of doing.
+ Noticing changes in taste or identity, such as clothing, an aesthetic or loving one type of food then hating it.
+ Finding things you have no memory of buying.
+ Experiencing gender dysphoria.

Confusion

+ Dissociating a lot, or being told you are.
+ Hearing other 'voices' inside your head or thoughts that are not your own.
+ Speaking like a child.

- Having chronic self-puzzlement and identity confusion.
- Noticing passive influence – feeling like your emotions are not your own.
- Your friends and family feeling like strangers, people who you do not recognise.
- Experiencing depersonalisation and derealisation, such as not recognising your reflection in the mirror, feeling disconnected to your body like it does not belong to you, the world feeling unreal or feeling like you are living in a dream.

Differences

- Noticing drastic changes in life focus.
- Having different career desires.
- Feeling shocked by your actions, such as feeling confused as to why you made an attempt to take your own life.

Memory Difficulties

- People telling you something that you do not remember doing.
- Having long and/or short-term amnesia, such as not remembering your childhood, having gaps in your memory or forgetting a particular skill or knowledge for a short time.
- Finding yourself somewhere unfamiliar and not knowing how you got there.
- Remembering childhood trauma, having flashbacks, body memories or other PTSD/CPTSD symptoms.

For advice for new and questioning systems, please see Chapter 10.

Overt and Covert Systems

There are two different types of DID and OSDD systems: overt and covert.

Overt Systems

Overt means not concealed, not secret but open to view. An overt system's outward presentation is more obviously multiple, therefore more noticeable by others. They display more obvious differences between each alter's physical presentation, such as changes in voice pitch, accent or fashion style.

Covert Systems

Covert means concealed or disguised. A covert system is a system whose switches are not obvious and whose presentation hides the fact they are a system. Covert systems are harder to spot than overt systems. Covert systems do not consciously decide to be covert. However, all systems may sometimes try to hide the fact they are multiple.

Some systems may sit in the middle of being overt or covert. Also, some alters may be more overt than others, such as child alters.

Are Overt or Covert Systems More Common?

Covert systems are a lot more common – at around 94 per cent. Richard Kluft, co-founder of the International Society for the Study of Trauma and Dissociation, observed 'only 6% make their DID obvious on an ongoing basis'.[1]

The representation of systems in the media suggests that all systems are overt and noticeable, and that each alter has very different outward presentations. This is not representative of the majority of systems. The general public and even some healthcare professionals are likely to have this misconception. Covert systems may have a harder time being believed by others.

Why Is It More Common for Systems to Be Covert?

Consider overt and covert systems within the context they exist. The current reality is that there is still a huge stigma against all systems, which is continually fuelled by damaging misrepresentations in mainstream media and a lack of understanding amongst mental health professionals. This means that existing openly as a system is inherently risky and could potentially be dangerous. This may be part of the reason why there are a lot more covert than overt systems. If DID and OSDD were more understood and accepted within society and the mental health system, perhaps systems would feel safer existing more openly.

Another possible reason as to why there are more covert systems could be the fact that DID and OSDD form out of the need for protection; therefore, being a covert system makes sense in the context of continuing to keep the system safe. Being more overt could put a system more at risk. Additionally, all systems may consciously or subconsciously conceal their multiplicity from others, such as by trying to prevent switches or acting in a way that is similar to the alter who people have met most often.

Polyfragmented Systems

Polyfragmented systems[2] are usually defined as systems that have over 100+ alters and have many fragments. Some people also use the term polyfragmented systems to refer to systems with subsystems and/or systems who have an organisation of alters which is complex. Polyfragmented systems are just as valid as non-polyfragmented systems. For polyfragmented systems, the recovery and therapy process may take longer and involve more layers of work compared to smaller systems.

Subsystems

Subsystems are distinct internal systems or groupings of alters within a DID or OSDD system. This can include situations where one alter has their own set of alters or where multiple systems exist within the broader system.

Inner Worlds

Some people with DID and OSDD have inner worlds. The inner world is also sometimes called the inside, the internal world or the headspace. An inner world is a space in a system's mind where alters can live and exist separately from the real world. It is like an imaginary world. Inner worlds can vary in size and be simple or very complex and detailed. Some systems experience their inner world visually, while others may sense it in emotional, auditory or more abstract ways. It can be a safe space for alters, often because the real world was unsafe. Over time, you may learn you have an inner world or learn more about your inner world. Some systems have areas of their inner world that hold memories or emotions and certain areas may only be accessible to specific alters. Additionally, some trauma holding alters may be hidden in specific areas of an inner world. Different alters have different levels of awareness or knowledge about their inner world than others. The inner world can feel quite special and private to some systems, so they may not want to share about it.

For some people with DID and OSDD, while alters are not fronting, they are living in the inner world. Their lives can be like life in the real world, detailed and rich. For some systems, alters in the inner world can communicate with each other. Some alters may have jobs in the inner world. There can be buildings, nature like forests, towns, cities, rooms, planets or fantasy places. Some alters have their own space in the inner world like their own house or room. The inner world can also change. The inner world can also be a valuable tool in therapy. It can provide a space for alters to connect, communicate and unburden themselves of trauma. You are just as valid if your system does not have an inner world or does not have a detailed inner world. Some systems try to develop, create, change or add to their inner world. One might do this by thinking 'It would be great to have a place in the inner world to have system meetings'. You could then visualise the type of place you would like, such as a green outside space, and change the visual image until you are happy with it.

System Shame and Guilt

It is very common for people with DID and OSDD to feel guilt and shame about having childhood trauma, being a system and being 'mentally ill'. They may feel that this makes them weak or unworthy. Shame can make systems scared to speak about their trauma or their difficult emotions. It perpetuates the secrecy of trauma. Shame can get in the way of systems telling others about their trauma or multiplicity for fear of letting them down. Shame can make systems hesitant to seek help. People with DID and OSDD may feel ashamed for being different from the 'norm' of singularity. Others may view multiplicity as wrong or less acceptable and trauma can deepen the belief that anything different is unsafe or bad. Over time, people with DID and OSDD can learn that it is not shameful to have trauma or be a system. It is the brain's clever and instinctual coping mechanism. Even though systems are misrepresented and underrepresented in the mainstream media, this does not make them shameful. People who love you will not reject you due to your trauma or multiplicity, they will support you and love you for who you are.

The stigma only perpetuates shame and guilt. Healthcare providers not understanding or believing these conditions plays into the shame and embarrassment. Many systems also carry the subconscious belief that the trauma was their fault, based on the assumption that bad things only happen to bad people. This is not true. Systems develop self-doubt and self-hatred as a protective mechanism from childhood trauma. Not understanding why they were hurt, they may subconsciously blame themselves, thinking they are the guilty one. This can result in feeling unworthy of happiness or love. Children are never to blame for their trauma. It was not their fault. They should never have been hurt. Over time, people with DID and OSDD can learn to accept that they do not need to feel ashamed and it was not their fault; this can also help them to feel less guilty.

System Responsibility

System responsibility means that systems are accountable and responsible for anything and everything an alter in their system does. If an alter does something wrong, then it is the whole system's responsibility. Being a system is not an excuse for getting away with things. You cannot put the blame on one alter. You must apologise and take responsibility for their actions. Most systems believe that it is a shared responsibility. This does not mean that individual responsibility does not exist. They both exist. It is important for systems to work together like a team. For example, if one alter raised their voice at someone, it is the whole system's responsibility to apologise.

Endogenic Systems

An **endogenic system** is a community coined, non-medical term used to describe a system that was not formed due to trauma. There is controversy regarding the existence and validity of endogenic systems, both within the DID and OSDD community and among mental health professionals. Professionals understand multiplicity through the lens of trauma and dissociation. An endogenic system is not a mental health diagnosis.

Some people believe that endogenic systems fit into the concept of multiplicity being a spectrum. However, endogenic systems are *not* the same as DID or OSDD systems and they cannot claim to be the same. The effects of a life tainted by trauma are very different from a life without trauma.

It is not uncommon for systems not to know about their trauma, and not remember anything traumatic when they first find out they are a system. They may believe that they do not have any childhood trauma and may be confused as to why they are a system. This is due to amnesia. The brain protects the child by compartmentalising the trauma memories, forgetting them because they are too overwhelming and difficult for a child to deal with. So, some systems may believe they are endogenic systems due to the fact they do not remember their trauma. However, over time these systems may start to remember traumatic memories, therefore making them DID or OSDD systems.

A **traumagenic system** is also a community term and not a clinical term. It refers to a system that was created due to childhood trauma, such as a DID, OSDD or P-DID system.

CHAPTER 8

Life as a System

Multiplicity Around the World

DID and OSDD are primarily diagnosed in European and North American societies. However, this likely reflects differences in awareness and diagnostic practices rather than true prevalence, as they may be underdiagnosed or misdiagnosed elsewhere. The article 'Dissociative identity disorder: An empirical overview' notes that 'DID is found around the globe in almost every culture...documented in Turkey, Puerto Rico, Scandinavia, Japan, Canada, Australia, the USA, the Philippines, Ireland, the UK and Argentina, among many other cultural and geo-graphical contexts'.[1]

In some parts of the world, mental health conditions are often dismissed or denied. This can include DID and OSDD. The medical and psychological framework is just one lens through which DID, OSDD and multiplicity can be understood. Multiplicity has existed across various cultures long before the development of Western psychology. Forms of multiplicity have been acknowledged in Indigenous, African, South Asian and other non-Western spiritual and cultural traditions. These are often framed as forms of spirit embodiment, ancestral presence or altered states of consciousness. It is important to recognise and respect the diverse cultural interpretations, experiences and histories of multiplicity. Not all cultures view multiplicity as pathological or disordered and these perspectives are equally valid and meaningful. In some places having multiple identities is seen as possession. While this may be celebrated in some cultures, in others it can result in alienation from the community and attempts to remove the possession, which can cause further traumatisation. In countries where there is less provision for mental healthcare or accessing this care is a luxury, systems can go 'untreated' for their whole life. Many systems will also not know that they are a system because this vocabulary is not present in their society. While life for systems can be hard everywhere, it is even more challenging in countries where a system's condition could result in them being shunned or banished.

All systems worldwide deserve understanding, acceptance, the option to define their multiplicity on their own terms and the option to access professional support, like therapy, if they wish to. In some cases, the option to define multiplicity in both cultural and psychological terms may require a country to accept that multiplicity can also be viewed as a mental health condition.

DID and OSDD in Children and Teenagers
DID and OSDD in Children
People generally find out that they are a system as an adult or sometimes as a teenager. This means that it is usually difficult to notice DID and OSDD in children. The covert nature of these conditions helps to protect the child. Typically, only adults receive a diagnosis. Some systems may be aware of their multiplicity at a young age, but may not know the language to express their experiences of multiplicity. In some cases, DID and OSDD in children may show up as other symptoms, such as mood swings, anger, amnesia or self-harm. Occasionally, some children or their carers may think a child has DID or OSDD. If this is the case, a mental health or medical professional should be promptly informed, allowing the child to get the appropriate help they need.

DID and OSDD as a Teenager
With the growth of social media, teenagers have become exposed to more information about mental health conditions, such as DID and OSDD. For some, this can result in teenagers realising and learning

that they are a system. However, a diagnosis of DID and OSDD is more common for adults. Learning you are a system as a teenager can be difficult. Learning you had childhood trauma is a lot to carry. You may fear not being believed for many reasons including your age or worry that others may assume you are making it up for attention. Others may think that your switches are just hormonal mood swings. The symptoms of multiplicity can get in the way of schoolwork or exams. It may also be harder to get a diagnosis. However, finding out you are a system as a teenager can have its benefits. The sooner someone finds out they are a system, the sooner they can start recovery, which should mean they will struggle with the manifestations of their trauma for less time. Systems usually find out that they are a system at the time that is right for them. If a teenager suspects they may have DID or OSDD, they should inform a teacher, mental health or medical professional to ensure they get the support they need.

Plural Pronouns

Pronouns are the way in which we refer to others. Examples of pronouns are he/him, she/her and they/them. Pronouns can reflect someone's gender identity. The singular they/them pronoun refers to one person. It is used by people who may not identify with she/her or he/him pronouns. People who use the singular they/them may be non-binary or gender nonconforming. They/them is considered a gender-neutral term. People with DID and OSDD may collectively use the singular they/them pronouns because these pronouns are gender neutral so therefore encompass all alters and their different genders. This allows for the alters who identify as male/female/non-binary and other gender identities to all feel included when being referred to, whether the person using the pronouns knows that this person has DID/OSDD or not.

Some people who have DID and OSDD use the plural they/them pronoun. It is used to refer to all alters at once. An example of this is 'My friend has DID and they are all so lovely. I'm seeing them this weekend.' Some people with DID and OSDD also use the plural pronoun we/we're, as a way to refer to all of their alters collectively, or several of their alters at once. An example is 'We have OSDD and we like being in nature'. When fronting, individual alters may use 'I' to refer to themselves and not any of the other alters. An example is 'I love to sew when I front. However, most of the other alters do not.'

Different alters can be different genders. They may prefer different pronouns to each other. They may ask you to use certain pronouns depending on who is fronting. Some alters may use the singular they/them pronoun for themselves. Some systems, such as large systems, may not ask others to learn each alter's pronouns. However, people with DID and OSDD may appreciate their therapist to use the right pronouns. Using the correct pronouns for different alters can feel validating and help reduce gender dysphoria.

TIPS FOR SUPPORTING PEOPLE WITH DID AND OSDD
If the system has informed you that they would like you to use different pronouns for them, you can ask for an alter's pronoun preferences. Do not worry if you get it wrong, apologise and then use the correct pronoun. For systems who just use one pronoun collectively, if you are unsure which pronoun they use, just ask.

Difficulties and Positives of Being a System

Each DID and OSDD system is different and will experience life differently. There is no one way to have DID or OSDD. Living as a multiple can be a lot more complex than living as a non-system. Multiplicity can greatly affect a system's ability to function in everyday life. Having multiple 'people' share one body has its challenges. Having different alters can mean having contrasting likes, dislikes, interests and desires. Having childhood trauma can mean flashbacks, body memories, getting triggered and amnesia. Everyday life as a system can be complex, confusing, exhausting and at times lonely. Systems can have an ongoing conflict between alters trying to sustain system functionality. Some systems may be able to work, and some may not. Either way, all systems are valid. Despite the difficulties, there can also be some positives of being a system and there are many ways in which systems can get help, which will be explored later on in the book.

Difficulties with Being a System
Alters

- Sharing your body with others
- Having a lack of system communication
- Finding it hard to make a group decision
- Alters wanting different lives to each other
- Being frontstuck (see Chapter 5)
- Switching and not being in control of who switches and when
- Alters having different and conflicting needs, interests, likes, dislikes and desires

Manifestations of Trauma

- Anxiety
- Confusion
- Hypervigilance
- Getting triggered
- Gender dysphoria
- Emotional intensity
- Finding change hard
- Exhaustion or fatigue
- Flashbacks and nightmares
- Self-harm and suicidal feelings
- Chronic pain and physical symptoms
- Long and short-term amnesia and losing time
- Dissociation, derealisation and depersonalisation

+ Depression, loneliness, emptiness and hopelessness

General Life

+ System doubt
+ The negative stigma
+ The long road to recovery
+ Wishing you did not have DID/OSDD
+ Learning you were traumatised as a child
+ Feeling shame, guilt, anger or sadness about being a system

Other People

+ Difficulty trusting others
+ Navigating relationships may be a little more complex
+ Feeling alone in your multiplicity
+ Difficulty navigating school/work/volunteering
+ Friends or family who feel like strangers at times
+ Difficulty of it being an 'invisible illness', which others cannot see
+ Some people, including mental health professionals, not understanding or believing you

Positives of Being a System
Alters

+ Feeling less alone
+ Inner system relationships
+ Your system feeling like a family
+ Having an internal support system
+ Knowing each alter developed to help you
+ Having multiple talents, abilities and interests
+ Experiencing happiness as a 'child' through littles
+ Being able to help each other, such as by switching
+ Alters being able to experience happiness for the first time

Trauma

- Knowing your system helped you to survive and keep you alive
- Usually only finding out about your trauma when your system is ready
- Having the trauma compartmentalised means that one alter does not have to deal with it all alone

General Life

- It is like a superpower
- Having fun in the inner world
- It keeps life from being boring
- Being able to collaborate to live life
- Living life through different perspectives
- Being able to re-watch films or re-read books
- Being more diverse like having a wide range of interests and tastes, e.g. in music

Other People

- Being attuned to others' emotions
- Being caring, sympathetic, empathetic and understanding of others
- Being good at adapting to different situations and getting on with different types of people

Birthdays as a System

All systems will have a day that they (the body) was born. This will be the system's date of birth. Some people with DID and OSDD may celebrate this day as the whole system's birthday. Even though the body will turn one year older each year, the ages of each alter in the system may stay the same. Not all systems celebrate their birthday.

Some systems have alters who have their own birthday on different days of the year. This may have been known or may have been chosen. Alters who do not age or alters who are children may dislike the body getting or looking older because they might relate to it less.

People with DID and OSDD who have not told others that they are a system or who do not speak about their system may find birthdays hard as they must pretend to be a non-system. It can also be hard for systems to decide who gets to front on their birthday and celebrating just one alter may make the others feel left out. Littles may get excited about presents but sad if none of them are toys or something they like.

How to Have a System Birthday

If possible, systems may wish to treat themselves to a few presents that they know multiple alters would like, such as a present for littles, for masculine alters and for feminine alters. Calling it your 'system birthday' can help it to feel more inclusive. In the inner world you could also have birthday parties and give presents to each other.

TIPS FOR SUPPORTING PEOPLE WITH DID AND OSDD
For friends and family of a system: you could ask if they would like presents for a certain alter or for multiple alters. An example is buying them a soft toy for the littles and then another present for the adult alters. You could also ask the system what name they would like you to use when you sing happy birthday to them.

Safety as a System

Systems are often more vulnerable and at risk than other people, for reasons such as amnesia, switching and having littles. Always be wary of your surroundings to help keep yourselves safe. Because of your added vulnerability and to protect your littles, you may want to consider additional safety measures such as not walking home late at night in the dark alone. Everyone in your system should be aware that they should never trust strangers and be prepared to remove themselves from an unsafe situation.

Staying safe as a system prevents further traumatisation and allows systems to focus on living their life. Systems may have a different relationship to safety than non-systems. This is because their safety was compromised as a child and now littles need to feel safe in the present. It is important for systems to be living and working/studying in safe environments; however, this is not always possible.

It is worth considering what things, people and environments make your system feel safe. This will be different for everyone – it's important to know what helps you. See the section Looking After Littles in Chapter 6 for ideas on how to make sure your littles are taken care of.

Dreaming as a System

Dreaming as a system can be different to dreaming as a non-system. Examples of this include:

Dream or Reality

- Some systems experience very vivid dreams.
- Dreams may feel very real or systems may mix up dreams with reality.
- Some dreams may take place in or be based on the inner world.
- Some systems may need more sleep than non-systems.

Who Dreams

- Some systems may dream collectively, some alters may share dreams and sometimes it may just be one alter who dreams.

- Systems may have dreams where alters are co-conscious or blended.
- Different alters may dream to the alter who was fronting most recently.
- Different alters may have different dreams in one night.
- Some alters may be in control of who dreams.

Alters

- Alters' dreams may look or be different to one another.
- Alters may be able to watch other alters' dreams.
- Alters may switch or rapid switch in dreams.
- Alters may experience different nightmares to each other or experience the same nightmare repeatedly.
- Different alters to the alter who went to sleep can wake up.
- Some systems or alters may not know which alter(s) had the dream.

Trauma

- It is common for systems to have trauma dreams or trauma nightmares.
- Systems may learn about repressed trauma memories in dreams.
- Systems may have body memories or flashbacks in a dream.
- Some systems may have a nightmare disorder.
- Some alters or systems may fear dreaming or falling asleep.

Discovery and Communication

- Alters may be told messages from other alters through a dream.
- Systems may meet new alters or dormant alters in a dream.
- Alters may communicate and interact with other alters in

a dream and see other alters who have their own separate body in a dream.

+ Systems may feel alters are a lot closer (to the front) before they go to sleep or as they are waking up, due to being in a semi-conscious state.

+ Lucid dreams can be a way for alters to communicate.

'Coming Out' as a System

Coming out as a system refers to telling others that you are a system. The stigma against DID and OSDD means that many systems will feel hesitant to 'come out' as a system to other people. It can feel scary and anxiety inducing. Systems do not want to feel invalidated, more vulnerable or unsafe. The current world is not designed for multiples but for non-systems. Navigating the world as a system can be challenging. However, being a system can also be a hard thing to hide and may feel like 'living a lie'. People with DID and OSDD differ in whether they choose to disclose their multiplicity. Remember that you do not have to. Take your time and only come out if you feel ready and comfortable doing so and know that it will not compromise your safety. If you want to tell others, or feel like it could be helpful to, begin by telling those closest to you who you trust. Some systems will only 'come out' if they have permission from all their alters to do so. However, this may be difficult to get. It can be helpful to have a system conversation or meeting with everyone to discuss the potential 'coming out', reasons for and against it and any concerns alters may have. If you tell others about your DID/OSDD, be prepared that you could potentially be met with responses that are unexpected or not what you wanted. Different people may react differently. Some may be confused, upset, overwhelmed, angry or in denial, while others may be supportive right away. If you decide to disclose that you have DID/OSDD publicly, you could potentially experience some life changing consequences, such as losing your job. This is discrimination but is sadly still something to consider.

How to Tell Others You Are Part of a System?

When you tell others that you have DID or OSDD, you may be asked, or decide to explain, what causes these conditions. Talking about childhood trauma may be difficult. Remember that you can say as little or as much as you like. You never have to disclose personal information about your trauma to anyone. If someone says 'so what happened?' you can reply with something like 'sorry I do not want to talk about it'. It is no one's right to know.

There are many ways to tell someone:

+ Tell someone **in person** in a conversation.
+ Send them a **message** or an **email**.
+ Tell them over a **phone call**.
+ **Write a letter** or a card explaining things.

+ **Ask how much this person already knows** about DID/OSDD/dissociation, before mentioning you are a system. This gives a better idea of where to start the conversation.

+ **Take things slowly** and gradually drop hints into conversation such as talking about dissociation.

+ **Give them this book or an information leaflet** on DID/OSDD and tell them 'this is what I have'.

+ **Some systems may refer to media representations** of DID/OSDD, such as the film *Split*, as despite it being a stigmatising portrayal it does give a reference point. If you do this make sure you mention that what you have is *like* the film *Split*, but not the same because you are not dangerous and this representation is inaccurate.

+ **An example of how to come out is** 'Hi, I don't know if you have heard of DID? It stands for dissociative identity disorder and it used to be called multiple personality disorder.

Well, I wanted to let you know that I have DID. I hope your perception of me does not change, I am still the person you know, there are just other parts to me. It is hard for me to tell you this, but I am telling you this because I care about you and would like to be honest. If you have any questions, feel free to ask.'

Telling others that you are a system can feel freeing and healing. It can also be helpful to have support from others who know what you may be going through, which can help you in your recovery.

You may also like to mention:

- that you refer to yourselves as 'we'
- how many alters there are in your system
- which alters this person has met before
- who is currently fronting
- signs of how you can tell another alter is fronting, e.g. wearing different clothes, different personalities, such as more confident or more shy, or different ways of speaking.

TIPS FOR SUPPORTING PEOPLE WITH DID AND OSDD

- If someone tells you they have DID or OSDD, thank them for sharing this with you.
- Believe them and do not doubt them, even if it feels difficult to comprehend.
- You may want to tell them that you are sorry that they experienced childhood trauma.
- Some people with DID and OSDD may not feel ready or comfortable speaking about being a system or their trauma. You might also find it difficult to talk about these topics and it is ok to take things at your own pace.
- If you have questions for them, ask if they feel comfortable answering questions about their DID/OSDD. If they

---

do not mind, try to take things slowly and try not to bombard them with too many questions. You could ask if there is any important information that would be helpful for you to know about their system or mental health. It is also ok if you do not feel comfortable asking questions.

- You could let them know that you would love to learn more about their system whenever they feel comfortable sharing.

- Sometimes being there for them is all they need. Try to not let this new information change your relationship. Continue doing the things you have always enjoyed doing together to show them that you still care about them.

- Try not to make a big deal out of them being a system and remember that not all systems are the same.

- Be careful not to invalidate their experiences and remember that people with DID and OSDD will likely know what they need better than you do.

- Remind them that you are always here for them and that you support them.

- Do not tell other people about this person having DID/OSDD, unless they have said it is ok for you to do so.

- Look after yourself. Learning that someone you know has DID/OSDD can be a lot to process. It is normal to feel overwhelmed, confused, upset or unsure about how to approach things. You may want to let the system know that it may take some time for you to process this new information.

What If No One Believes Us?

It may take others some time to process that you have DID/OSDD. This is normal. Multiplicity can be a confusing concept for people to try to grasp at first. It can also be hard for people close to you to learn and accept that you experienced trauma as a child. It may be upsetting and they may blame themselves for not noticing or not know how to respond. No one wants to learn that someone they love has been through traumatic experiences as a child. Hopefully, over time, they come to accept this. Educating them could help, such as by giving them this book to read or talking more about what DID/OSDD is. Allow people the space and time to accept that you are a system.

Some people may find it hard to accept and they may be in denial. They may find it easier to convince themselves otherwise. It may be the case that they still do not believe you even after some time has passed, or still believe that DID/OSDD do not exist. Remember that even though they do not believe you, this does not mean that you are not a system. You know yourselves best and know what you have experienced. Maybe one day this person will come around. In the meantime, you could try telling someone else, telling a mental health professional or engaging in the online system community. You deserve support and you deserve to heal.

If a medical or mental health professional does not believe you this can be hard too. If possible, try and speak to another health professional or find one who understands DID/OSDD/trauma/dissociative disorders. Professionals not believing systems usually comes from a lack of knowledge.

Analogies for Multiplicity

Using analogies or similes can be a helpful way to try to explain multiplicity to others. Analogies describing one whole that is made up of multiple parts include:

+ a jigsaw puzzle
+ a patchwork quilt
+ a disco ball
+ a satsuma
+ light through a prism
+ kintsugi
+ a stained glass window
+ a constellation

✦ the solar system.

Doubts and 'Faking'
Are We Faking It?
Systems often wonder if they are faking being a system. It is very common to question this, so do not be alarmed. Systems may be doubtful due to societal disbelief, a lack of societal education and awareness, the negative stigma, skeptical professionals, comparing themselves to the stereotypical image of an overt system or doubting that their trauma was 'enough'. If you are worried you are faking it, it probably means you are not. You would know if you were making it up. You cannot pretend you are a system without consciously being aware that you are pretending. It would also be a difficult thing to fake.

System Doubt
It can be hard accepting that you have DID or OSDD, whether you have a diagnosis or not. Having system doubt is very common. Some alters may find it harder to accept that they are part of a system than others. Littles may be more accepting that they are part of a system compared to adult alters. Each alter may have to go through their own journey of acceptance, which may take a while; this is ok. The amnesia between your alters allowed you to survive, so the knowledge that you have other alters may seem strange, scary, unexpected and difficult to accept. Over time system doubt can lessen and may even disappear.

How to Help with System Doubt

✦ **Ask yourselves why you think/thought you were a system in the first place.** The fact you questioned whether you are a system is important and a sign that you may be.

✦ **Gather all the evidence.** Have a space where you compile all the examples that you are a system; this could be written as a page in your journal or on a computer document. Examples could include other alters buying something that you do not remember buying, having different handwriting, different alters having their own clothes, changes in how you speak, examples of amnesia and reminders from your friends/family/therapist of your changes in behaviour.

+ **Communicate with each other.** Communicate in forms that you can look back on to remind you that you are part of a system, such as writing notes to each other in your journal or leaving voice or video messages on your phone.

+ **Be aware of the societal doubt.** The stigma against DID and OSDD presented by society can make it harder to accept you have it.

+ **Interact with others.** Connecting with other systems online or in real life is a great way to meet people just like you and can feel validating. It can make you realise that you are not making it up because there are many other systems out there with similar experiences.

+ **Diagnosis.** If you are a diagnosed system your diagnosis can act as validation that you *are* a system. You went through a lengthy and thorough assessment. These diagnoses are not handed out easily. If you are an undiagnosed system, getting a diagnosis may help with system doubt (if accessible).

+ **Time.** Over time your system doubt is likely to lessen. As you get used to being a system it begins to feel more normal. If you are in therapy, the amnesic walls between different alters may begin to break down, which can help lessen doubt.

+ **Ask yourself: Why would you be making it up?** You know

that being a system is not easy, it is complex and can make you feel like no one understands you. It can make life more difficult in a society set up for non-systems. Few people would wish for this or wish to have childhood trauma.

Not knowing you are part of a system was a protective coping mechanism to help keep you safe. It is normal to doubt yourselves. Almost all systems experience system doubt.

> **OUR EXPERIENCE**
> *When we first got our DID diagnosis, we had some system doubt and questioned whether we were faking it. However, over time this has reduced and we now know for certain that we are a system, whether we like it or not! Therapy has definitely helped us with this, although we sometimes sometimes experience moments of doubt.*

Wishing You Were a Non-System

People with DID and OSDD may hate or dislike the fact that they are systems. They may wish they did not have DID or OSDD. It may be all or just some of the alters in a system that feel this way. Life as a system brings its difficulties. Alters who feel this way may just want a less complex, easier and more stable life. The negative stigma of DID and OSDD is another reason why systems may wish they were a non-system. They are not understood by the majority of society. This can feel isolating, frustrating or sad. Systems may wish they were never traumatised as a child. They may feel envious of non-systems and envious of people who do not have childhood trauma. Life as a system can be hard and it is completely understandable and valid to have all these feelings. Over time, in recovery, these feelings may lessen.

People with DID and OSDD must remember that without the clever coping mechanism of your personality not fully integrating and creating alters, you may have not survived. Your alters saved you, and ensured that traumatic memories were forgotten, allowing you to get on with everyday life. Systems' brains are intelligent. Systems are special and unique shape shifters. Systems are like superheroes.

CHAPTER 9

System Organisation and Communication

System organisation and communication are two helpful ways for alters to learn more about their system. Neither require therapy, so they are accessible to everyone.

System Journals

Journalling is a great way to find out what you are actually feeling and why you may be feeling this way. It is like a form of therapy. Writing down your thoughts can help you to make sense of things, gain clarity, reduce anxiety and help you come up with solutions to your problems.

Some systems have a system journal. This is a place where alters can communicate with each other, log switches and note down everyone's thoughts. Some alters may not mind writing in the same book, other alters may prefer to have their own journal – do whatever works best for you. You can find a notebook(s) that you like or find a specific DID/OSDD journal. The author of this book has also published a journal for systems, titled *The DID & OSDD Journal: A Guided Journal for Organising Your System and Supporting Your Recovery Journey*, which serves as a perfect accompaniment to this handbook. The journal includes alter profiles, switching logs, timeline pages, crisis plans, pages for littles and more. It provides a valuable resource for system documentation, discovery and functionality.

Keeping your system journal safe and private is important. You may want to think about where to keep it so that others you live with do not come across it, while remembering that all your alters also need to know where to find it. Leaving a note in your phone of where you keep your system journal can be helpful for alters who do not know or cannot remember.

What to Include

Many systems like to include specific pages at the beginning of their system journal, such as a list of all of your alters, system rules, journal rules, a page for leaving notes to other alters and a page at the very beginning to say *if you are not [insert name of the body/system name] or an alter in this system do NOT continue reading, this is private!* It may also be important to include trigger warnings on journal pages or notes to advise littles not to read certain pages. However, this could tempt littles, so having a rule that other alters cannot read each other's journal entries may be more helpful. It could be helpful to have a dedicated notebook, computer document or journal page where you list a timeline of your life, including when your trauma happened. You could also have a page where you document your trauma in more detail; however, this is not essential and could be triggering.

OUR EXPERIENCE

Keeping a system journal has been invaluable for us. Having all our system information organised in one place is incredibly helpful. It's great to be able to reference our list of alters, read detailed alter profiles, use specific pages for system communication and journal our thoughts and feelings on life. We also make a habit of journalling before and after every therapy session. This helps us to prepare by reminding us of topics we want to address and document any realisations or insights from the session. Journalling has played such an important role in our recovery journey, and we would greatly recommend it to all systems.

System Mapping

System mapping refers to how alters relate to each other and how a system functions and is structured. Mapping your system, alters, inner system relationships and the inner world can be helpful and insightful. Some systems draw paper diagrams, some make digital diagrams, some make collages, some use Pinterest boards, some use toys and some even create their inner world in 3D, such as in The Sims.[1] A mind mapping/spider diagram technique can also be used to help map a system. Some systems just prefer to write a list of their alters. System mapping can help to show which alters are connected to each other, such as alters who are aware of each other or alters who are similar to each other, e.g. introverted alters. System mapping can involve documenting the alters who front most often or those who are aware of trauma. It can include timelines, such as a timeline of when each alter was first discovered. Mapping an inner world can involve documenting where different alters live and what it looks like. It may also be helpful for people with DID and OSDD to show their system map to their therapist.

System Communication

System communication can be split into two different categories: internal system communication and external system communication. Internal communication goes on inside your head/mind/headspace/inner world. External communication takes place outside of your mind, in the real world. Communicating as a system can help you in your recovery. The thought of system communication may seem scary, confusing or feel difficult at first, so just take things slowly, keep practising and try one form at a time to see what works best for you.

You can communicate internally by:

+ accepting all of your alters and creating a welcoming space. Letting them know that you care about them and that they are all equally important

+ speaking to other alters while you are in the inner world
+ speaking to other alters inside while you are fronting, through your thoughts or inner monologue. Such as *'Good morning everyone'*, *'Good night everyone'*, *'I'm really proud of you all today'*, *'How are you all doing today?'*, *'Is someone feeling upset?/ Who is feeling upset? It's ok to feel sad'*, *'Why are you feeling scared?'*, *'What would you like?'*
+ asking (simple) questions inside to others like *'Do you have a favourite colour?'*, *'Do you like this?'* (E.g. while looking at a flower)
+ addressing a particular alter; using their name can help get their attention. E.g. *'Hey Samantha, are you there? I was just wondering if...'*
+ communicating through images, words, feelings, body sensations and your intuition
+ trying visualisation or guided meditation to talk to others
+ talking to alters in your dreams
+ hosting a system meeting (see below)
+ making announcements to your alters, such as allowing them to speak in the headspace whenever they would like or letting them know they can interject while you are journalling.

You can communicate externally by:

+ speaking out loud to the alters inside
+ leaving voice messages or video messages to others
+ writing letters, notes, sticky notes or cards to each other
+ using a group chat app and 'texting' each other when different alters front (e.g. Simply Plural)
+ journalling; some systems have a shared system journal which can be a place to communicate with others through writing. This could be through leaving notes for others to read in the future or having written conversations by writing down what everyone is saying internally in the present moment

- collaborating, such as inviting different alters to draw, paint or write together
- asking someone like a friend or therapist to speak to a specific alter and ask them questions.

System Meetings

System meetings are a form of system communication. They are an organised meeting held by one system for the alters in their system. It can be between two or more alters; sometimes the whole system may attend. The purpose of a system meeting is to discuss important issues regarding the system. Not all alters may want to be present or be able to be present, such as being in a different location in the inner world. However, alters that cannot attend the meeting 'in person' may be able to still hear the meeting and contribute.

System meetings help organise a system's life and they can be a good place to hear other alters' views. They can also act as a place for the system to vote on decisions, for example, if one alter wants to dye the body's hair a different colour they can bring this request to the system meeting to see if the majority of the system agrees. Some systems will get alters to vote on these decisions and only go through with it if there is a majority.

It is up to systems to decide how they would like to run their meetings. It may not always be appropriate for littles to attend and they may get bored. It can be helpful to organise for an alter or two to look after the littles during a meeting, or let them play instead.

Some systems may find it difficult to have system meetings and others may be scared to try and organise one. To start a system meeting you could make an announcement to your system in your inner world. You could say something like 'Hello everyone, I hope you are all doing ok. I was thinking that it could be useful to try and have a system meeting. I was thinking we could do it today at 5pm. It would be great if you all could join. There is no pressure if you do not want to though. Hopefully see some of you there!' In system meetings, alters will usually speak in the inner world, not out loud in the real world.

You may want to nominate an alter to take notes of the meeting; this could be the alter who is currently fronting so that the notes are in the real world. It can be helpful to find a quiet place in the real world for your meeting. Systems may also find or create a safe, friendly space in the inner world where they can have their system meeting. Some systems invite everyone to sit in a big circle in the inner world so that everyone can see each other.

CHAPTER 10

Advice for Systems

Advice for Questioning Systems
If You Think You May Have DID or OSDD

It is ok to be intrigued or question whether you may have DID or OSDD. It means you are being proactive in recognising a mental health condition that you could potentially have. Everyone who has DID or OSDD, whether diagnosed or not, will have discovered that they are a system in different ways, including resonating with symptoms, experiencing severe dissociation, being told by a professional they may have a dissociative disorder, watching a documentary on these disorders or remembering childhood trauma. It may not be obvious at first, but the whole point of these conditions is for the amnesia to hide the fact you have different alters. For a list of signs you may be a system, please see Chapter 7.

Tips for Those Who Think They May Have DID/OSDD
Curiosity

- Continue to be curious about why you think you are a multiple.
- Document all the reasons and examples as to why you think you are a system, such as creating a list of alters and alter profiles.
- Continue to educate yourself about DID, OSDD, trauma and dissociation.
- Do not go digging into your past to try and remember trauma without professional help, as this could be dangerous.

Diagnosis

+ Look at the diagnostic criteria.
+ Have a look at diagnostic screening questionnaires online (see Chapter 21 for more information).
+ Consider an assessment for dissociative disorders. or speaking to a medical professional who can advise you on the path to a diagnosis in your country.
+ Be wary of jumping to a self-diagnosis too quickly. Take time to understand your experiences fully.

Other People

+ Speak to family and friends about it if you feel comfortable, such as asking if they have noticed any changes in your behaviour.
+ If you are already receiving help for your mental health such as seeing a counsellor or therapist, voice your thoughts; mention that you think you may have a dissociative disorder. If you are not seeing a mental health professional speak to your GP/primary healthcare provider.
+ If someone tells you they do not think you have DID or OSDD, but you still think you do, this can be hard. Continue to be curious and document your experiences.

Management

+ Find some self-regulating, self-soothing or grounding techniques that work for you (see Chapter 25).
+ Create a crisis plan (see Chapter 24) and give copies to people that you trust, if you are able to.

Advice for New Systems

Finding out you are a system may feel scary, overwhelming or confusing, and that's a completely natural response. Remember that you are not alone. There are millions of other systems out there who understand. Finding out you are a system may also bring up other emotions like relief, validation or sense of resolution and that's ok too.

- Give yourselves time to process. Do not rush to find out more.
- It is ok if things feel a little bumpy at first. You may not know who is fronting. Over time, you will learn more about your system.
- Do not try to remember your trauma or worry about why you are a system, you will find out naturally when the time is right.
- It is normal to go into denial, have doubts or feel ashamed that you are a system.
- There is no rush in telling others that you are a system.
- Respect other alters' feelings and privacy, such as do not share information about them online or with others without their permission.
- Your system may 'grow' as you find out about other alters. This is ok.

Advice for All Systems
What Can Help?

- Having a routine, like waking up at the same time each morning, can help to keep everyone in your system feel on top of everything.
- Research, read educational books (see Recommended Resources at the end of the book), watch documentaries and, if interested, connect with other systems when you feel ready to.
- Pace yourselves with learning new information about DID/ OSDD. If it is overwhelming, take a break or take things more slowly.
- Get to know everyone in your system, such as through

creating a list of alters' names, creating alter profiles, having system meetings or logging switches (see Chapter 5).

+ Journalling is a great way to process your thoughts. You could also create a system journal to help collate all of your system information (see Chapter 9).

+ Using plural pronouns like they/them and we/we're can help you to feel more connected to your system. Some systems just like to use plural pronouns in therapy, while journalling or while thinking. Other systems may also ask the people in their life to use them too.

+ Some systems like to set alarms on their phone throughout the day as a reminder to check in with their system and to prevent long stretches of dissociation.

+ Communication within the system will get easier if you work on it.

+ If possible, try and find a therapist who works with people with DID and OSDD. (There are some therapist directories in the Recommended Resources section.)

Remember

+ You are not broken.
+ You are not faking.
+ You are the ones who are the experts on your system.
+ All systems are different.
+ Learning that you share your body with other alters can feel overwhelming, but they are all you. Try to love them all. They helped protect you and helped you to survive.
+ Unfortunately, people may tell you that you are faking it or that DID and OSDD are not real. This can come from a place of misunderstanding, a lack of education or stigma, and is not a reflection of you.
+ Things will get better and easier over time.
+ Be gentle with everyone in your system; everyone is trying their best. Be kind to yourselves.

CHAPTER 11

Understanding and Accepting Trauma

Accepting Your Trauma

Accepting you have childhood trauma can be hard. Initially it may be a shock to find out. It can then take time to accept and some might not want to accept it. It is ok to feel this way. Accepting your trauma does not mean that you forgive the people that hurt you. Acceptance and forgiveness are different. Acceptance means accepting that it happened. It does not mean that it should have happened or that it was ok. Some systems may decide to forgive the people that hurt them while other systems do not. However, you do not need to forgive the people who traumatised you in order to heal. How a system decides to process their trauma and feel towards the people that hurt them is up to them.

Trauma Survivor?

Not all systems may feel comfortable identifying with the term *trauma survivor*. The label may feel restrictive. Systems are more than a trauma survivor and they can thrive after trauma, not just survive. However, to some systems it may feel empowering, a reminder that even though they went through trauma, they survived. Sometimes, trauma survivors are called *victims*. Some people with DID and OSDD do not like this term, as it can feel disempowering and shameful. Instead, people may prefer other terms such as *warrior*. Be hesitant with using these different labels when referring to systems. It can be helpful to check if they are ok with these phrases before you use them.

What If I Do Not Remember My Trauma?

People with DID and OSDD will not always know about or remember their trauma. Some systems may learn more as they get older and others may never know the full story. People with DID and OSDD may have also experienced multiple traumas; these may be remembered at different times in their life. OSDD-1b systems who have little or no dissociative amnesia may have more awareness of their trauma memories than systems with DID or OSDD-1a.

Many systems only remember their childhood trauma when they are adults because the brain blocks out the trauma memories to protect them. This is called dissociative amnesia. The dissociative amnesia allows the child to get on with everyday life. People with DID and OSDD may only uncover memories of trauma in therapy or when triggered. Trauma memories can also show up as body memories or emotional memories rather than visual memories or memories they can put words to.

Additionally, in one system, some alters may know what trauma the system experienced and some may not. A system may feel like they have no trauma; however, individual alters may implicitly or unconsciously withhold trauma memories to help protect the system. Other alters may have no access to these trauma memories or have no awareness of the alters who do.

Not remembering childhood trauma or not being aware of it can make getting a DID or OSDD diagnosis harder. If you do not remember your trauma, it is important not to force yourself to remember. Your system knows best and will begin to reveal information when you are ready. If your current circumstances are traumatic or unpredictable, then your system may delay bringing childhood trauma memories into awareness until you are in a more stable and safe environment. Many therapists still work with undiagnosed systems or systems who are not aware of their trauma.

Is My Trauma 'Enough'?

Some professionals may believe that people with DID and OSDD's trauma must involve repeated sexual or physical abuse, occurring before a certain age in childhood. This is not the case. If you have a trauma related disorder, then your trauma *was* enough. Each person's window of tolerance for trauma is different. Your trauma is valid regardless of what it was or how much trauma you have. It is common for systems to feel like their trauma was not enough. They must remember that they were traumatised as a *child*. This is very different to experiencing trauma as an adult. Children lack the life experience and coping mechanisms that adults have and their brains are not fully developed. Children are more vulnerable and have less capacity to cope with extreme stress and trauma. If you developed DID or OSDD then your trauma was 'enough'.

Trauma and the Body

Trauma can be stored in the body as well as the mind. Many manifestations of trauma are felt in the body, an example being body memories. The body can remember what the mind might not yet be able to. For people with DID and OSDD, therapy helps to heal the mind. Systems may also wish to engage in additional practices to help heal their body. If you are interested in learning more, there are many books dedicated to this subject, some of which are included in the Recommended Resources at the end of this book.

Traumaversaries

A traumaversary is the yearly anniversary of someone's trauma. Even if someone consciously does not remember what happened or *when* their trauma happened, their body can remember. This can affect the particular date(s) that the trauma took place in the year, as well as the days around it. Holidays, religious celebrations and traditions may also be triggering to some systems, such as the festive season or Halloween. On a traumaversary, people may experience body memories and flashbacks, feel exhausted or feel scared. To help, try to look after yourselves and do simple self-care tasks. Take things slowly, tell yourselves that you are safe now and that this will pass. If things get more difficult, look at your crisis plan (see Chapter 24). Some systems come to learn when their traumaversaries are in the year, so may take time off, take things more slowly or show themselves more compassion.

This Trauma Has Ruined My Life

Having childhood trauma, especially if you have DID or OSDD, may mean that your life looks different to people who do not have childhood trauma. Systems may feel like their life is ruined. But it is not. You can live a fulfilled life *despite* your trauma. Try not to let your trauma dictate your life. It is not in control of you. You are powerful and capable. It is completely possible to live a 'normal', happy and fulfilled life. Getting help through therapy is the best way to heal, allowing your system to live the life that they want.

Telling Other People Your Trauma

You do not have to tell *anyone* about your trauma, even if they ask. If you choose to share, it is best to tell someone you trust and feel safe with, such as a friend, family member or therapist. Only tell someone if and when you feel comfortable and remember that you never have to give any details if you do not want to. For some, talking about trauma in therapy can be helpful and healing. You may also find it beneficial to let trusted people in your life know that you experienced childhood trauma, but you do not have to say any more than that. Speaking about your trauma can be difficult and may even be triggering. If you tell someone, you may want to let them know you told them in confidence and that you would appreciate it if they do not tell anyone else. You are never required to tell mental health professionals the details of what happened to you, even if they ask. The only time it could be helpful is during an assessment for dissociative disorders. If you are aged 18 or under and tell a professional about your trauma, such as a teacher, they may have a safeguarding duty to take action or tell someone else about it.

Reporting Your Trauma

If applicable, some people with DID and OSDD may decide to report their trauma to the police, such as reporting their abuser(s). For some systems, this can feel helpful or empowering and it may prevent the abuser from harming other children in the future. It is never too late to report something to the police. If you decide, make sure that you are in a stable enough place to do so first and have someone to support you with it. If it ends in a court case, you may have to give evidence in front of a jury and your abuser(s) may be there. This could be a triggering experience. All countries have different procedures for reporting someone to the police and the stages that follow.

It is ok if you do not feel ready to report someone, there is no rush. It is also ok if you do not want to report someone to the police. The most important thing is to prioritise your system's safety.

There are many charities that are able to offer advice and support regarding reporting someone to the police. They may be able to assist you and offer an advocate for free. (See the Recommended Resources.)

Traumatising Living Environments

Sadly, some people with DID and OSDD continue to live in environments that are highly stressful or traumatic. This can cause systems to live in a constant fight/flight state and can result in more alters being created. If this is the case, systems should prioritise staying safe in the present, rather than trying to recover. Examples of this are living with abusers, being bullied at school or having frequent interactions with someone who is triggering or dangerous. If possible, systems should try to leave traumatising situations, for example by moving in with trusted relatives or changing schools. However, this is not always possible for a variety of reasons, such as teenage systems not being able to enact this change themselves.

If you are a system living in a traumatic situation, please know that you deserve so much better. It is not your fault. Things can get better. If you can, speak to someone you trust, such as a teacher, school counsellor, friend, helpline, the police or your HR department, and let them know about your situation. Your safety is the most important thing. If you are under 18 years old and tell someone what is happening, they may legally have to pass it on for your safety. Safeguarding laws will differ between different countries.

Dealing with Your Abusers

Some people with DID and OSDD may still be in contact with their abuser(s). This could be daily, occasionally or unpredictably. This is a difficult and triggering situation to be in. Some systems may have always known who abused them and others may have only found out recently, due to dissociative amnesia. If possible, try to avoid coming into contact with your abuser(s). However, this may not always be possible. Some systems decide to report their abuser(s) to the police. Others decide to relocate so they do not have to come into contact with them. Some systems decide to change their appearance such as dyeing or cutting their hair so they are less recognisable. The priority is to keep yourselves safe.

CHAPTER 12

Remembering Trauma

Flashbacks
What Is a Flashback?

A flashback is a vivid re-experiencing of a past event, such as trauma. They are sudden, unexpected and can be distressing, often feeling as if the trauma is happening right now. Flashbacks are unprocessed memories. Your mind does not realise that the trauma is a memory. They can last for a few seconds or continue for several hours or even days. Not all flashbacks are visual. Flashbacks can involve images, body sensations, pain, smells, tastes, sounds or emotional memories related to trauma. They can be triggered by anything such as certain places, people, objects or situations. Sometimes it may not be clear what triggered a flashback. Flashbacks from childhood trauma can result in littles fronting, being closer to the front or getting triggered. Flashbacks can replay the traumatic memory in your mind like a movie or like a slideshow of photographs or quick flashing images. Flashbacks can bring traumatic memories to conscious awareness that systems were previously unaware of. This can be overwhelming and scary. For some systems they may feel like nightmares while they are awake. For OSDD-1b systems who typically have little or no amnesia, flashbacks may be more experienced and remembered by most or all alters, which can be difficult to deal with.

Triggers

A trigger is when something external reminds you of something from your past, triggering a memory, such as a reminder of past trauma. Triggers can involve all five senses: sight, smell, sound, touch and taste. A trigger may lead to a flashback or a body memory and can result in alters presenting more overtly. There can be 'positive' triggers and 'negative' triggers.

- ✦ **Positive triggers** may be happy memories from a system's past and cause a certain alter to front. An example of this would be *in system X an alter called June is fronting, June sees a football and this may positively trigger an alter in their system called Ray who loves football, which could cause Ray to front.*

- ✦ **Negative triggers** can be reminders of a system's past trauma. It may not be obvious as to why something is triggering to a system due to amnesia. Experiencing a trigger can be challenging and overwhelming. An example of a negative trigger is *system Y had medical trauma and going into hospitals or hearing beeping sounds can be triggering for them.*

Over time, systems may learn what can be triggering for them. Different alters may also have their own triggers. If a system talks about being triggered they are most likely referring to being negatively triggered. In society or on social media some people refer to being triggered as a joke. This is not something to joke about.

It is important that systems do not share their negative triggers with anyone who could use it against them or to manipulate them. It may be helpful to tell people close to you, who you trust, what your triggers are so that they can help you to avoid them. Systems may also find it helpful to write down a list of their triggers for themselves. Through therapy, systems may find they get triggered less often and become better equipped to cope with triggers.

> **TIPS FOR SUPPORTING PEOPLE WITH DID AND OSDD**
> Avoid speaking about topics that could be triggering; if you are unsure, just ask.

Body Memories

Body memories, body flashbacks and emotional memories are implicit memories stored in the body. When recalled they can feel like you are experiencing a past trauma in the present moment, even though they are memories being a memory from the past. Body memories are physical rather than visual memories, experienced as a physical sensation or feeling in the body. The body remembers what the mind cannot. A body memory can happen as a result of being negatively triggered, which reminds the system of a past trauma. Body memories can also be triggered by the five senses. Systems may or may not know why they are having body memories or what triggered them. Even if a system's trauma was not physical, the trauma can still be stored in the body. Often body memories are the first type of trauma memory a system experiences.

Body memories can be unpleasant to experience. The physical sensations can be intense or terrifying. Having no words or visual memories to explain these sensations can feel confusing. Body memories can make you feel powerless, helpless and like you are trapped. They can cause you to freeze, feel nauseous or stop you from being able to speak. They can cause panic similar to a panic attack. Body memories can make you feel unsafe or as if your body is unclean. Body memories may also make systems want to escape their body or get out of their skin because being present in their body is too unbearable. Systems may also experience psychosomatic pain.

Some body memories can be of positive past experiences, although this is less common. These positive body memories can be pleasant, such as a system remembering running on a beach as a child. It is the body memories from difficult and traumatic experiences that can be especially challenging to manage.

Body memories can be so overwhelming that systems may have to leave work/school/the place they are currently in. This is ok. Looking after yourselves is important.

Body memories can last from a few seconds to a few minutes, hours or more. Systems may engage in unhelpful behaviours to try to stop body memories such as harming themselves. They may also become suicidal or dissociate. However, there are healthy ways to help deal with body memories.

How to Cope with Flashbacks, Triggers, Body Memories and Remembering Trauma

Remembering trauma, whether through flashbacks, triggers or body memories, can be extremely difficult, painful and challenging. Often the memories come from child alters, which is helpful to keep in mind. Different coping mechanisms work for different systems and alters. You might find it useful to bookmark this chapter so you can easily return to it when needed. Here are some things to try:

♦ **Take yourselves to a safe environment.** It may help to find somewhere private if you are not at home, such as a bathroom in your school or workplace or going outside. If you are outside, you could find a bench, park or just go home. If things become too overwhelming wherever you are, you can always leave. If you are somewhere you cannot leave, ask to speak to your school nurse/counsellor/boss/line manager. If it is not possible for you to leave at that time, remember that you can go home soon.

♦ **Remind yourselves that you are safe.** Tell yourselves 'We are safe now. The trauma is over. Even though it feels like it is happening right now, this is just a memory. This is just a flashback. It is [insert year]. We are not in danger. We are in an adult body now. This too shall pass. This will be over soon. We will get through this.' Look around at your surroundings and notice that you are in the present and not the past. Note the objects you see out loud or in your head, such as our bookcase, our table, our comfy chair, our pen... You can also remind yourselves of what year it is by looking at the date on your phone.

✦ **Comfort yourselves.** This could be by curling up in a blanket or in bed under the covers, hugging a soft toy (plushie), cuddling a pet, listening to soothing music or birdsong, having a warm drink like tea or lighting your favourite candle. You may also feel comforted by being in the presence of loved ones, doing the butterfly hug, or soothing and reassuring yourselves, such as telling the trauma holders 'I'm so sorry you experienced trauma. This never should have happened. It was never your fault. You deserved so much better. We are safe now. We are here to protect you.'

✦ **Distract yourselves and engage in an activity you like** such as watching your favourite film or television show, reading a children's picture book, eating your favourite food, baking cookies, colouring-in, playing gentle sport, doing a jigsaw puzzle, playing a video game, going on a walk, spending time in nature or going to your favourite museum.

✦ **Treat yourselves.** Buy yourselves a nice drink, your favourite snack, a magazine, an easy dinner or some flowers.

✦ **Try to keep yourselves safe.** You may have alters who want to act on dangerous or harmful thoughts. Do everything you can to avoid this from happening, such as following your crisis plan (see Chapter 24), staying at home, returning home if out or staying with loved ones. Some systems also find visualising a safe space or going somewhere safe in their inner world helpful.

+ **Reach out to others** in your system through internal communication or a system meeting. You could see if there are any alters around that could help or switch, such as a protector. It could also be helpful to speak, call or message your friends, family, therapist, colleague or a mental health crisis line. You may want to tell them you are having a flashback, remembering trauma, are not feeling good, just want to talk or you may just want to have a conversation about something more general. You do not have to give details about what is happening.

+ **Focus on your breathing.** When you are frightened you might stop breathing normally. This increases feelings of fear and panic, so it can help to concentrate on breathing slowly. Breathe in like smelling a flower and breathe out like you are blowing bubbles. Breathing out for longer than you breathe in helps to calm down your sympathetic nervous system. For example, breathe in for 4 seconds, hold your breath for 4 seconds, then breathe out for as long as you can (e.g. 6 seconds) and then repeat.

+ **Go to sleep.** If a flashback feels too overwhelming or you feel exhausted, have a nap or go to bed early. This helps take your mind away from the experience and allows you to get some rest. It can also be helpful in preventing a crisis.

+ **Try to continue with simple self-care** such as eating three meals, drinking some water and brushing your teeth. Keeping a routine will be helpful.

+ **Take a break** or some time off work/school/your regular activities or responsibilities. Cancel plans if you need to. Have a mental health rest day if helpful and possible.

◆ **Try grounding techniques.** These help keep you connected to the present, which is important. Some examples include looking for circles in your surroundings, having a shower, hugging someone, holding an ice cube, feeling different textures around you or eating something sour or spicy.

◆ **Carry an object that reminds you of the present.** Some people find it helpful to touch or look at a particular object during a flashback, such as a small pebble or toy. This might be something you decide to carry in your pocket or bag, or something you have with you anyway, such as a keyring or a piece of jewellery.

◆ **Avoid your triggers** and avoid watching or being in environments with quick flashes such as certain television shows or dark concerts with flashing lights.

◆ **Make notes.** It can be helpful to journal your thoughts and feelings during or after these experiences. You could write or draw how you feel. Understanding your triggers is important. It can be helpful to write down a list of your triggers, although be careful when doing this. This can help you to avoid them, not forget them and allows you to bring them to therapy to explore and unpack. Therapy is a safe space to explore and work through your triggers and flashbacks.

◆ **Try some gentle movement.** Wiggle your fingers and toes, shake your limbs, try some gentle movement like stretching, yoga, jogging inside or hugging yourselves.

CHAPTER 13

Emotional Challenges

Emotional Intensity

People with DID and OSDD can experience strong emotional intensity. Individual alters may experience intense emotions and there can also be multiple, simultaneous emotional reactions, such as one alter who feels angry and one alter who feels depressed at the same time. It is also not always easy to identify who is feeling what emotion. Having multiple responses can be overwhelming and tiring. However, it can be helpful to recognise that often these strong emotions are your alters trying to communicate. Try asking inside why they are feeling this way or what you could do to help them. Child alters may be getting triggered; be curious about this. Unblending from these alters allows you to stop and look at the situation, help to reduce the emotional intensity and find solutions.

Depression

Depression is common for people with DID and OSDD and can be difficult and distressing to experience, with many possible causes. For some, it may stem from the psychological and emotional challenges of living as a system with a history of childhood trauma. For others, it may also function as a subconscious coping mechanism, a way the mind shuts down or withdraws to help protect itself from further pain.

Depression can be debilitating and hard to shift. It may also cause guilt and shame. It can make systems isolate themselves from others and make anxiety worse. It can make everything seem grey, make life feel hopeless and can sometimes lead to systems having a crisis, such as thoughts of ending one's life or making an attempt. Even though these feelings can be overwhelming, they will not last forever. Support is available and there are ways systems can help themselves and begin to heal.

How to Cope

- **Ask who is feeling depressed.** In a system, the person fronting may feel like they are the one who is depressed as they are experiencing the feelings, emotions or physical symptoms of depression. However, this may be passive influence, the depression belonging to another alter(s). Finding out who is feeling depressed can be helpful as it allows you to try to help them. You could ask in different ways such as by broadcasting it in the inner world or having a conversation in your journal.

- **Distraction can help.** Even though you may feel like you do not have the emotional or physical energy to engage in a task, distracting yourselves can provide a helpful break. Start off with small tasks. Try engaging in activities that your system enjoys such as baking, gardening or reading. You could also engage in something fun like watching funny videos, looking at memes or watching a comedy film.

- **Get outside.** Try to get some fresh air once a day. This could be standing outside or going on a walk. It may help to listen to a podcast or music while walking.

- **Achieve something.** Achieving something each day can make you feel accomplished and proud. It does not have to be something big. Examples include doing one thing on your to do list, cooking dinner, having a shower, making your bed, doing the laundry, texting a friend or going on a walk.

+ **Journalling is like a mini therapy session.** Try writing just a line or two or doing a 'brain dump'. Writing how you feel can help you work out why you feel this way and how you could help yourselves. It can feel like a release getting it all out. You could also paint or draw how you feel. This can be therapeutic and may be easier and more enjoyable for the littles.

+ **Tell someone.** Telling someone you feel depressed, or if you do not want to use that word, honestly telling them you do not feel the best, can feel like a sigh of relief. Systems may fear feeling like a burden, but those who care about you will support you and want to help. Being honest with how you feel with others can also help you to accept how you feel, making it easier to help yourselves.

+ **Try a gratitude list or achievements, closeness and enjoyment log (ACE log).** Writing one thing that made you happy each day can help you see that there are moments of happiness in your day despite your depression. Alternatively, you could write down what you are grateful for or list some moments that were nice that day. An ACE log is similar, you write down something you Achieved, a moment of Closeness and something you Enjoyed in your day. It can help when you are feeling depressed to focus on the small moments of joy.

+ **Look after yourselves.** This can be hard but it can help you to feel a little better. Try to achieve the 'simple' self-care tasks such as brushing your teeth, showering, making your bed and eating three meals a day. Even if the alter fronting does not want to do these things for themselves, ask them to do it for the rest of your system. Sticking to a routine can help with this. Praise yourselves for doing these tasks.

◆ **Reach out if you need more help.** If there is a mental health professional you can talk to, let them know how you are feeling. It is also important to reach out if you are in crisis or fear a crisis may be nearby. If you do not have any professional support, see if you can get some help and, in the meantime, call a mental health helpline or contact your GP/ primary health provider.

◆ **Doing something you enjoy** such as going to an art gallery, meeting up with a friend, treating yourselves to a coffee, listening to music, cycling, playing the piano, sketching or trying something new.

◆ **You may wish for someone to switch** with you if you have fronted for a while or feel as though you are no longer able to cope with the depression. Is there someone else who would be willing to front?

◆ **Have a spring clean or organise your bedroom/house.** Getting rid of clothes or items that you no longer need and donating them to charity can feel freeing and help you feel lighter and good about yourselves. You could pick one place to organise such as your desk draw or your wardrobe. Just make sure you do not throw something away that belongs to or is liked by another alter.

◆ **Is there something triggering you?** Have a think or ask to see if any alters are being triggered by anything in your day-to-day life, such as a depressed alter being triggered by a depressing book or an alter who fears an upcoming life event.

◆ **Connect with others.** Even if it is just a quick text message to a friend, a phone call, video call or a quick meeting for a coffee or a trip to the cinema.

+ **Allow yourselves rest.** It is ok to feel depressed. It is ok to take things easy and rest. Also make sure you get enough sleep.

+ **Help others.** Such as by volunteering, checking in on a friend or donating clothes to charity.

+ **Change.** If you know why you are feeling depressed then you may wish to change something in your life to help, such as finding a less triggering job or applying for a volunteering role to help give you a sense of purpose. Changing something can also feel new and exciting. Set small and realistic goals. It may help to ask: what advice would you give to your friend if they were in your situation?

OUR EXPERIENCE

Like many systems, we can experience depression. It can come in phases and feel completely all-consuming and hard to escape. When we realise that we are depressed, we try to find out why; there is always a reason. We will be curious about what we have been feeling and thinking about. We will also be curious about what has been going on in our life which could have caused us to feel depressed. We will ask inside to try and find out which of our alters is feeling this way. We know that some of the alters in our system are more prone to experiencing depression or have very heightened emotions. Discussing how we feel in therapy is a great way to find out why or who feels this way. Being honest to the people we know about how we feel can really help lift some of the depression, which can be such a relief. Whether we know the cause of our depression or not, we then see if there are any changes we could make. We are extra kind to ourselves when we feel depressed and know that engaging in work and personal projects always helps us as a form of distraction and helps us to feel accomplished. We will also comfort, praise and validate our

> *system. At the end of each day, we write down at least one nice thing that happened that day, such as hearing birdsong, laughing with others or seeing a cute dog. Noticing the little but special everyday glimmers can feel restorative.*

Anxiety

Anxiety is an emotion. It is feeling worried, panicked, fearful, stressed or feeling a sense of dread. Everyone can experience anxiety to varying degrees; however, for some people it can affect their everyday life. It is common for systems to experience anxiety linked to their childhood trauma. Trauma can keep systems to be on high alert in everyday situations, often putting them in a fight/flight state; this is known as hyperarousal. However, anxiety can also be influenced by other factors such as genetics, brain chemistry and current life stressors.

Each system and each alter in a system can experience anxiety differently and in varying intensities. Anxiety as a system can be complex, the body may experience physical sensations of anxiety, yet it may be unclear who the anxiety belongs to. In one system, some alters may not experience anxiety at all and other alters may have debilitating anxiety. Some systems may be diagnosed with an anxiety disorder and some may not. If you have not been diagnosed with anxiety, your anxiety is just as valid as someone who has a diagnosis.

There are different types of anxiety, including:

+ agoraphobia
+ generalised anxiety disorder (GAD)
+ health anxiety
+ obsessive compulsive disorder (OCD)
+ panic disorder
+ phobias
+ social anxiety disorder.

What Anxiety Can Look Like for Systems
Physical Symptoms

+ Tight chest
+ Fast heart
+ Shaky limbs
+ Light-headedness
+ Difficulty breathing
+ Compulsive behaviours
+ Intense unpleasant body sensations
+ Panic attacks that can be a result of getting triggered

Psychological Symptoms

+ Rumination
+ Fear of people
+ Fear of the future
+ Fear of leaving the house
+ Fear of getting hurt (again)
+ Constant worry or overthinking
+ Having nightmares or flashbacks
+ Being in a constant state of hyperarousal

Anxiety can result in:

+ isolation
+ difficulty sleeping
+ fear of trying new things
+ depression and loneliness
+ turning down opportunities.

How to Cope
See Chapter 25 for general coping tips and advice.

Locate the Anxiety

+ See if you can find out who is feeling anxious, such as by asking inside.
+ See if you can find out why this alter is feeling anxious. Is there anything you could do or say to help them with this?
+ Journalling may help you find out why you feel anxious.

Finding Support

+ Try opposite action (see Chapter 25).
+ Remember that you are not alone in feeling this way.
+ Talk to friends/family/a therapist/a doctor about how you are feeling.
+ Let others know that you experience anxiety or that you are currently feeling anxious.
+ Doing trauma work in therapy for your DID/OSDD can help to reduce your anxiety.

Panic Attacks

Many people with DID and OSDD experience panic attacks, which may or may not be related to their trauma. Panic attacks can feel scary, especially for littles and alters who have not experienced them before. They usually last from five to 20 minutes; however, they can last up to an hour or more. Panic attacks can be triggered by a variety of situations, such as after a flashback or during a time of extreme stress. Systems may not always know why they are having a panic attack. Some systems may also be diagnosed with panic disorder.

Symptoms of a Panic Attack

+ Sweating
+ Tight chest
+ Feeling numb

- Fear and panic
- Racing heartbeat
- Feeling nauseous
- Shaking or trembling
- Feeling faint or dizzy
- Feeling hot or feeling cold
- Freezing, not being able to move
- Dissociation, depersonalisation, derealisation
- Finding it hard to breathe, having very quick breaths like a pant, shallow breathing, having large gaps between breaths or feeling like you are choking

How to Cope
See Chapter 25 for general coping tips and advice.

Medication?

- Some systems may find anti-anxiety medication helpful.
- Some systems may find CBD (a chemical found in cannabis that has no psychoactive effect but does have some medical benefits) calming.
- Medication is not essential for panic attacks.

Grief
Grief is a natural part of life and something everyone will experience. You should not be ashamed for grieving. Everyone experiences grief differently. This can mean that different alters in a system may experience and process grief differently, even for the same event. Alters may grieve many different things including the death of loved ones, pets, relationships ending, friendships ending, their past or the childhood they should have had, free from trauma. Grief is not always related to death.

Different events may lead to different types of grief. An event that came as a shock may be grieved differently to an event that was expected. However an alter decides to grieve is ok, as long as the system stays safe.

There are differences in grieving as a system; some alters may:

- process more quickly, some more slowly
- go into crisis or harm the body
- go into a trauma response (e.g. freeze)
- dissociate
- forget about the situation entirely due to amnesia
- consciously push it aside and try to continue with everyday life
- feel intense emotion
- feel numb
- stop regular plans
- distract themselves
- stop fronting
- go dormant
- grieve in the inner world
- not want to believe what happened
- split.

Grief may be particularly hard for littles. This could be because they remain at a childlike stage and have not learned the ways to handle difficulties yet. They have not had the same life experience as the older alters. Grief or difficult events that lead to grief may also be triggering or feel unsafe to littles. It is important to look after littles when alters or the system is grieving.

How to Cope

- Be patient, grief can be a long process and that is ok.
- Be kind to yourselves.
- Try different forms of processing such as making art about how you feel, journalling or writing a letter to the person/thing you are grieving.

+ Take time off if needed and take things slowly. Focus on one hour at a time or one day at a time.
+ All your emotions related to grief are valid, like guilt, anger and sadness.
+ Make sure everyone in the system is ok, such as by having a system meeting (see Chapter 9).
+ Keep yourselves safe.
+ It can feel like it is the end of the world but over time things *will* get a little easier to manage.
+ Speak about your feelings with friends/family/therapist or get help from your GP/primary healthcare provider.
+ Ask for help if you need it.

CHAPTER 14

Behavioural Responses

Unhealthy Coping Mechanisms

People with DID and OSDD may consciously or subconsciously use certain coping mechanisms to help cope with difficult feelings. Some of these coping mechanisms can do more harm than good in the long term, even if they feel like they are helping in the short term.

Unhealthy coping mechanisms can become a habit, which can be hard to break and may turn into an addiction. Realising that a behaviour is an unhealthy coping mechanism is a great first step, as it allows you to slowly work towards changing it. In some cases, you may need professional help with this.

Unhealthy coping mechanisms can impact you in many ways, such as affecting your finances, affecting your mental and physical health and affecting your relationships and ability to work. They can include:

- gambling
- aggression
- self-harming
- overworking
- social isolation
- excessive screen time
- shopping addictions or overspending
- abusing/over-consuming/relying on drugs or alcohol

- being promiscuous – if used as a form of self-harm or to escape reality
- avoiding problems or denying problems exist and suppressing emotions
- engaging in dangerous behaviours, such as breaking the law or trespassing
- controlling eating, such as binging, restricting, overeating, emotional eating or only eating safe foods
- dissociation: a coping mechanism that protects systems during childhood. However, deliberately engaging in dissociation when you are not in immediate danger can make the habit harder to break and make it more difficult to stay present in reality.

Self-Harm

Self-harm is when someone or an alter deliberately harms themselves. This could be physically or psychologically. It can become an addictive, secretive and dangerous behaviour. Sadly, it is not unusual for people with DID and OSDD to self-harm. An article in the *Australian and New Zealand Journal of Psychiatry* noted: 'Self-harm and substance abuse are typically found in over 50% of people with DID.'[1]

There are many different forms of self-harm, which will not be listed here for the safety of those reading this book. Some systems have certain alters who engage in self-harm. If alters in your system self-harm it can be helpful to explore why they do so.

Reasons Systems May Self-Harm

- To manage difficult emotions or trauma
- To cope with depression or hopelessness
- To turn emotional pain into physical pain
- To release tension or stress

- To reduce dissociation, to feel 'real' or feel less numb
- To feel in control
- To punish themselves or express shame/guilt
- To express anger or frustration
- To communicate distress (to others or within the system)
- To feel cared for or comforted (even subconsciously)
- Because it was learned as a coping strategy
- To avoid more serious harm or attempts on their life

System-Specific Tips for Coping with Self-Harm

- Work out who wants to self-harm.
- Talk with the alter who wants to self-harm. Find out why they want to self-harm. Do they need anything?
- Ask the alter who wants to self-harm to switch with someone else, if they cannot promise not to self-harm.
- Get another alter to switch or be co-conscious if the current alter cannot keep the body or system safe.
- Check in with your whole system. Ask inside: does anyone know why there is an urge to self-harm? Was there a trigger?
- Show compassion. Let them know that you are sorry that they feel the need to self-harm. Thank them for trying to help the system.
- Explore healthier ways to cope together and create a list of safer alternatives, which can also be shared with loved ones if that feels helpful.

Getting Help for Self-Harm

People with DID and OSDD who self-harm deserve to get help. Telling someone you trust that you self-harm (and that you would like to stop or reduce this behaviour) is a good place to start. You could tell a medical or mental health professional such as a counsellor, therapist, general practitioner doctor (GP) or primary health provider, teacher, school nurse, friend, family member, guardian or a work colleague. You may feel reluctant to tell others as you may feel ashamed, guilty or embarrassed. However, this is not what the other person will think, they will just want you to be safe. It may seem daunting but it can help you to feel less alone. Remember to only tell someone if it is safe for you to do so.

Getting Urgent Care for Self-Harm

It is important for systems to seek urgent medical care for self-harm if it is severe and needs medical attention. The best option is to go to your nearest accident and emergency/emergency room (A&E/ER). It is also helpful to know how to care for yourself if you do not need urgent medical attention. Having a first aid kit on hand can be useful. Unfortunately, some healthcare professionals assume that people self-harm for attention; this belief is damaging and is rarely the case. There can be a multitude of reasons as to why people self-harm, and if it is for attention, it could be a subconscious cry for help. People who self-harm are hurting.

Alternatives to Self-Harm

When systems have self-harm urges, they may feel driven to act in harmful or reckless ways towards themselves. However, there are many alternatives that are less risky and dangerous; these include:

Touch

♦ Holding ice on your skin where you wish to self-harm
♦ Having a cool shower or warm bath

Sight

♦ Drawing red marks with pen, makeup or paint on your skin where you want to self-harm
♦ Putting stickers or temporary tattoos on your skin where you want to self-harm
♦ Placing plasters (band-aids) where you want to self-harm

Taste

+ Chewing gum
+ Cooking or baking something

Change Something

+ Dying your hair a different colour
+ Painting your nails
+ Styling your hair in a fun or unusual way
+ Rearranging or organising a room

Release Energy

+ Running as fast as you can on the spot, down your road or in a park
+ Punching or screaming into a pillow
+ Doing star jumps (jumping jacks)

Self-Reflecting

+ Journalling why you want to self-harm
+ Writing down all your feelings, emotions or difficulties on a piece of paper and ripping it up

Distraction

+ Painting, drawing or playing a video game
+ Making a pillow fort

Comfort

+ Watching cute animal videos
+ Buying or hugging a soft toy (stuffed animal)

Disordered Eating

It can be common for people with DID and OSDD to struggle with eating or have difficulties in their relationship with food. This could be because it brings a sense of control or comfort. Systems may also experience disordered eating due to their relationship to their body. Issues with eating may feel all consuming. For people with DID or OSDD, it may be one or several alters who have difficulties with eating, rather than the whole system. However, this can impact the whole system. It is important that the body remains healthy so that system recovery is possible.

Eating difficulties can include restricting, binge eating, making yourselves sick, overeating, undereating, or only eating certain foods.

Issues with eating in a system can be complex. There may be various reasons why alters struggle with food, such as only eating foods that littles like or choosing 'safe' foods that do not trigger memories of their trauma. Understanding the underlying cause can help the system move toward a healthier relationship with food.

Some systems or alters may also have (diagnosed) eating disorders. If this is the case, or is thought to be the case, it is important to seek professional support. Challenges with eating may make systems feel ashamed but you deserve understanding and support. Caring for the body is important.

How to Cope

+ Tell someone you trust.
+ Speak to a professional if it is impacting your everyday life.
+ Try to eat three meals a day.
+ If you are hungry, allow yourselves to eat.
+ Try to eat enough for the sake of the littles. They deserve enough food and for your adult body to be fuelled and satiated.
+ Slowly work on reducing harmful eating behaviours.

153

- ✦ Recognise that engaging in these behaviours could be a coping mechanism in response to your trauma.
- ✦ Remember that having issues with eating does not make you a bad person.
- ✦ Know that you can change your relationship with food for the better.

Alcohol and Recreational Drugs

Mind altering substances, including alcohol and recreational drugs, can be harmful to systems, especially if they are overused, abused or relied upon. People with DID and OSDD may have alters who drink or or use drugs to cope with difficult emotions or as a form of self-harm. Though this may seem to help in the short term, it may often make things harder in the long term and can negatively affect the entire system.

One alter may want to drink or use drugs, while others may not want to, especially the littles. Alcohol and drugs may increase vulnerability, disrupt internal communication and make recovery more difficult. These substances can also make relationships with others more challenging and may leave the system feeling less safe and connected, so be careful. If you notice an overreliance on these behaviours it may help to explore safer alternatives.

If you do engage in alcohol or drug use, be aware of the potential risks and consider whether gradually reducing consumption might be helpful for your system. You may want to ask yourselves why you are engaging in these behaviours. Are you trying to escape reality, a feeling, avoiding tasks, blocking out flashbacks? Working on these underlying reasons in therapy can help reduce the need for drugs or alcohol.

If the system is of legal drinking age and has a healthy relationship with alcohol this is generally safer. Keep in mind it can still affect your system, particularly littles, so try to drink slowly and safely. Everyone has different views regarding drugs and alcohol. What matters most is your system's safety, health and recovery.

CHAPTER 15

Cognitive Challenges

Memory and Amnesia

People can experience memory loss in different ways, from ordinary forgetfulness to more severe amnesia and trauma-related dissociative amnesia. Amnesia refers to any type of memory loss, whereas dissociative amnesia specifically refers to memory loss that is related to trauma or extreme stress. People with DID and OSDD can experience all of these types of memory difficulties.

In childhood, dissociation causes all systems to develop amnesia of their trauma. This allows them to continue living their everyday life and stops them from being overwhelmed by trauma memories. As adults, amnesia is often experienced by people with DID and OSDD-1a. Amnesia in systems is more complex and often more severe than typical forgetfulness. It can be scary and difficult to live with.

Systems with dissociative amnesia may have periods where they cannot remember information about themselves or events from their past. They may not remember their trauma, alters or (parts of) their childhood and some memories may only be accessible to certain alters. These blank episodes may last minutes, hours, days, months or years. Systems can experience long-term amnesia, short-term amnesia, amnesia between different alters and individual amnesia. Regardless of whether the memories are 'good' or 'bad', the brain may block access to them out of fear of them being unsafe or triggering.

Amnesia may cause a system doubt and confusion. An example

155

of a system experiencing amnesia is 'Our system cannot remember much of our past at all, whether yesterday, a couple of weeks ago or a couple of years or decades ago. This is very scary and sad. It really impacts us all.'

Some OSDD systems may experience less amnesia and have more access to everyone's memories compared to DID. OSDD-1a systems typically have more general dissociative amnesia or fragmented memories but often experience less amnesia between their alters because they are less distinct. OSDD-1b systems who have more distinct alters do not experience amnesia between their alters. However, both OSDD-1a and OSDD-1b systems can experience dissociative amnesia for trauma.

Memory = Life?

Having little to no memory can make systems question what defines them as a human. Are our memories and past experiences what make us human? Having little to no memory may make systems feel more present in the present, as this is the only reality they occupy, as they are mostly unable to live in the past.

Repercussions

Amnesia can put strains on relationships and affect every aspect of life, such as making it difficult to:

+ work, study at school, college or university, or take exams
+ remember daily tasks like eating or taking medications
+ remember to pay bills
+ remember to attend appointments
+ read books and remember what you previously read.

Getting Your Memory Back

Systems with severe amnesia may feel like they have dementia. It is not dementia. Memories can return, whether 'good' or 'bad'. Through the right therapy, over time, the dissociative walls can begin to break down, making it easier to access and share memories.

However, this should never be forced, it will happen naturally when the time is right. You *can* get your memories back and your memory *can* improve.

> **OUR EXPERIENCE**
> *Before we were diagnosed with DID, a therapist we had would get angry at us when we told them we could not remember what happened in our week. They would raise their voice at us. They would not believe us and insisted again and again to try to get answers from us. We wanted to remember but could not. It made us feel inadequate and sad and compromised the therapeutic relationship, breaking the trust. Another therapist could have noticed this severe memory loss as a sign of dissociation. We changed therapists after this repeatedly happened.*

TIPS FOR SUPPORTING PEOPLE WITH DID AND OSDD
Be understanding that systems may have amnesia and memory issues, such as when they switch.

Coping with Amnesia/Memory Loss/ System Organisation Tips

+ **Jot down notes** – write down important things to remember on sticky notes or in a notebook, such as a reminder to attend an appointment. Stick them somewhere where all alters will see.

+ **Use alerts** – create calendar alerts on your phone or computer for important things to remember, such as alerts every evening for medication and for therapy appointments.

+ **Phone calendar** – put in key dates and appointments into your phone or computer calendar. This way it is always with you and may be easier for you all to find.

+ **Paper diary/calendar** – put in key dates and appointments into a paper calendar diary. This can be used in addition to your phone calendar app. It can be easier to see what is happening in the upcoming week.

+ **System journal** – a good place to leave notes for other alters or find out what others have been up to. You may want to put 'Private' on entries that you do not want other alters to read.

+ **To-do list** – write a daily to-do list to make sure you get everything done. Keep it out so other alters can see it. Tick or cross out completed tasks. Examples on a to-do list: shower, take medication, write essay, food shop.

+ **Tell someone** – like a friend or family member, as it will make it easier to remember. You can also ask them to remind you of it. Speaking it out loud can help too.

+ **Therapy** – through therapy memories can become more integrated. This can help with both long and short-term memory.

How to Cope with Depersonalisation, Derealisation and Dissociation

Depersonalisation and derealisation are both symptoms of DID and OSDD. Depersonalisation is the feeling of being detached from your body and derealisation is the feeling of being detached from the world around you. For more information on these experiences see Chapter 1.

Ways to Cope in the Moment

- Try to remain calm. These experiences are a normal part of having DID and OSDD and should pass soon.
- Be curious as to why you may be feeling depersonalised, derealised or dissociated. What triggered this? You could ask inside to see if anyone knows. It is likely that these responses are trying to protect you from something stressful, such as feeling scared. Are your littles ok?
- Try some grounding techniques (see Chapter 25 for some ideas).
- Remind yourself what year it is and look around at your surroundings and list what you can see.
- Keep yourselves distracted, such as by continuing your day-to-day activities, organising your kitchen cupboards or calling a friend.
- Comfort yourselves and find ways to help relax such as by having a warm drink, hugging yourselves or putting on comfy clothes.
- Have a change in scenery.
- Breathe slowly and deeply.
- Say some positive affirmations.
- Try a short, guided mindfulness or meditation exercise.

Ways to Cope in the Longer-Term

- Learn about the ways which help your system cope with stress.
- Keep a regular routine, such as sleeping and eating at the same time each day.
- Learn more about depersonalisation, derealisation and depersonalisation.
- Track these experiences and what causes them on a log.
- Talk to a therapist about these experiences.
- Therapy for your DID/OSDD can help your depersonalisation, derealisation and dissociation lessen over time.

CHAPTER 16

Physical Health

Comorbid Conditions

People with DID and OSDD can also have other mental and physical health conditions, which is very common. These can be both diagnosed and/or undiagnosed.

Living with DID and OSDD can be exhausting. Having physical illnesses on top of this can be even more exhausting. It can feel like you are constantly trying to get better or constantly in survival mode. Being unwell mentally and physically all the time is difficult. Many systems experience physical illness as a manifestation of having trauma.

Systems may also have:

- depressive disorders
- anxiety disorders (such as generalised anxiety disorder or obsessive compulsive disorder)
- personality disorders (such as borderline personality disorder)
- eating disorders (such as bulimia, anorexia nervosa or binge eating disorder)
- body dysmorphic disorder
- physical conditions (such as chronic pain or chronic fatigue syndrome).

Systems may also have traits of some disorders, or episodes such as:

- paranoia
- disordered eating

- panic attacks
- psychosis
- flashbacks
- suicidal ideation
- self-harm
- mania
- phobias
- sleep problems
- anxiety
- depression.

OUR EXPERIENCE

Living with trauma can be exhausting. Just getting through the day is a huge accomplishment. We also have chronic fatigue and chronic pain. These can be debilitating and can prevent us from engaging in everyday life. Trauma can contribute to these kind of physical health challenges.

Increased Risk of Physical Illness

Childhood trauma means that systems are likely to have experienced and may still be experiencing high levels of stress. Chronic stress can increase the risk of developing physical illnesses such as digestive issues, chronic pain and chronic fatigue. Many systems have also experienced adverse childhood experiences (ACEs) and some studies have found people with multiple ACEs may have an increased risk of cancer.[1] To reduce the likelihood of developing serious physical illness, systems can find ways to help reduce their stress. See Chapter 25 for some ideas.

TIPS FOR SUPPORTING PEOPLE WITH DID AND OSDD
Remember that systems can get tired more easily than non-systems and may also experience additional health conditions.

CHAPTER 17

Intersectionality

Intersectionality is defined as 'the complex, cumulative way in which the effects of multiple forms of discrimination (such as racism, sexism, and classism) combine, overlap, or intersect especially in the experiences of marginalized individuals or groups'.[1] It is important to consider how aspects of a system's social identity can result in variations in privilege and discrimination, such as within the system community and within the medical field. This can include a lack of access to assessments for dissociative disorders, difficulty with receiving treatment for DID/OSDD, a lack of support, a lack of acceptance and representation in the system community and a lack of support and acceptance from the system's friends/family/guardians/classmates/colleges/medical and psychological professionals.

The factors which can influence discrimination against systems can include: race, ethnicity and nationality, gender, money, politics, stability of the country one resides in, disability, religion, neurodiversity, sexual orientation, age and class.

Discrimination exists against all systems due to the stigma surrounding DID and OSDD; however, aspects of a system's social identity can cause a much greater level of discrimination. It is important for everyone to be aware of intersectionality and how it manifests with those who have DID and OSDD. If you witness discrimination against a system, stand up for them. All systems deserve to be treated equally and all systems are valid regardless of their social identity.

If you are discriminated against in your school, college, university or workplace, if you feel safe to do so you may want to report it.

If you experience discrimination outside of these places there are a few things you can do such as: ignore it and/or distance yourselves from this person/people or speak to someone close to you about it. It is not your job to try to educate others; however, you can try to if you would like to. Ignorance is not an excuse for discrimination. Be wary that some people may not be open to changing their views. The most important thing is to keep your system safe.

BIPOC Systems

BIPOC stands for Black, Indigenous, People of Colour. BIPOC systems face g difficulty when it comes to being a system compared to white systems. BIPOC systems' experiences are very different from white systems' experiences. Racism, discrimination, prejudice and microaggressions exist in many forms and greatly amplify a BIPOC system's struggles. It must be noted that this book is written by a white system. Though the author has spoken to BIPOC systems who have helped to inform this book, it may still not fully represent BIPOC systems' experiences and we encourage and support alternative resources. We thank those who have kindly contributed their time to help inform this book.

As racism can exist in any situation, BIPOC systems will have increased difficulty in many areas of their life compared to white systems. Examples include BIPOC systems finding it more difficult to get a job or to access governmental benefits and assistance due to racism. This leads to more stress as a system and more adversity.

Racism exists in the medical field. BIPOC systems are more likely to be discriminated against, mistreated and judged. They are more likely to be offered a lesser level of care in general hospitals, psychiatric inpatient and outpatient hospitals, within therapy and within doctors surgeries. BIPOC systems may face more challenges accessing help such as accessing therapy and getting a DID or OSDD diagnosis. They are more likely to have their experiences invalidated by medical and mental health professionals and denied help. BIPOC systems may also experience more system doubt and their recovery journeys can be more complex and take longer than white systems'.

Intergenerational trauma, including slavery, racial segregation and racism, exists for BIPOC systems. Historical trauma does not mean that BIPOC cannot develop DID or OSDD.

BIPOC systems can find coming out as a system more difficult. They can find it hard to ask for help and can experience more fakeclaiming. BIPOC systems are more likely to be taken less seriously than white systems. BIPOC systems may feel like there is not a space for them in the online system community and therefore feel excluded. Their views are less likely to be heard. Importantly, BIPOC systems' perspectives should not only be sought when it comes to discussing race-related issues.

People cannot claim to understand multiplicity, DID and OSDD without the consideration of BIPOC systems' experiences. Researchers cannot claim to understand multiplicity or have gathered a representative sample size without gathering information from BIPOC systems. Mental health professionals cannot claim to understand multiplicity without having worked with BIPOC systems.

Things need to change. BIPOC systems deserve to feel seen, heard and supported in all of their experiences.

What Can Help BIPOC Systems?

- ◆ Connecting to other BIPOC systems, such as on the online system community.

- ◆ If possible, you may prefer to find a therapist/psychiatrist who is also BIPOC as they will understand your experiences.

- ◆ Having an advocate in medical situations, such as having a professional advocate or someone close to you who you trust who can help stand up for you.

- ◆ If you feel comfortable you may want to call out others on their racism, such as making a complaint to your local mental health provider. However, this is not your responsibility, so you do not have to do this. You can also get support from advocacy services when making a complaint. Examples in the UK include The Patient Advice and Liaison Service (PALS) for the NHS, and charities like Citizens Advice, VoiceAbility and Victim Support.

♦ Know that your experiences are just as valid as those of white systems, and you are equally deserving of support and care. You are important, worthy of compassion, understanding and a safe space to heal and thrive.

What Can White People/Systems Do to Help BIPOC Systems?

White people, especially white systems and white mental health professionals, need first to be aware of the inequalities that exist and to acknowledge that the blame for those inequalities lies with white people. White systems need to be aware of their privileges that BIPOC systems do not have. They have less to deal with than BIPOC systems. White systems need to be aware of cultural appropriation and not invalidate BIPOC systems' experiences. They must show sympathy and care towards BIPOC systems. White systems need to actively ensure they are anti-racist in their life. **There are lots of ideas about how to be a good ally online, including Investing in Ethnicity's toolkit.**[2]

White systems need to do more for BIPOC systems. BIPOC systems need greater representation in the online system community and their voices need to be lifted by white systems. It is vital that systems of all races are heard and represented fairly.

Alters of Different Races

There has been some controversy in the system community regarding systems having alters who are of different races, such as a system in a white body having an alter of colour. Alters cannot choose their race and some alters that are a different race to the body may be introjects. However, what matters is how these alters describe their experiences. Even if an alter identifies as a different race, they are still not truly of that ethnicity and cannot fully understand what it is like to be of that ethnicity or culture. They do not understand the history of BIPOC and cannot claim it as their own. They do not experience the real-world discrimination, prejudice and racism faced by BIPOC individuals and claiming such experiences can be harmful to BIPOC systems. Conversely, BIPOC systems can also have alters that are white, but these alters can still experience racism because they inhabit a body that is not white.

LGBTQ+

The acronym LGBTQ+ stands for lesbian, gay, bisexual, transgender and queer. The + is used to be inclusive of other sexual or gender identities.

It is common for a system to have alters with diverse identities in terms of gender, romantic preference and sexual orientation. For example, in one system there could be alters who are straight, bisexual, asexual, aromantic, male, female, non-binary and transgender. All alters are just as valid regardless of how they identify. Heterosexual and cisgender alters are not more valid than alters who identify as being LGBTQ+. Living as a system who has alters that identify as LGBTQ+ may be difficult or confusing, such as when different alters have different preferences for romantic relationships.

Systems can also be transgender and some transgender systems choose to medically or socially transition. Systems may face more difficulty in the healthcare system with trying to transition, due to their multiplicity. Some alters may also gender slide, meaning their gender identity changes over time or across situations.

All alters deserve love, acceptance and the freedom to be who they are. Your system's unique diversity is beautiful and deserves to be celebrated.

Gender Dysphoria

Gender dysphoria is the feeling, discomfort or distress that can occur in people whose gender identity differs from their sex assigned at birth. Gender dysphoria is common in systems that have alters who are a different gender to the sex their body was assigned at birth. Gender dysphoria can be emotionally painful. Feeling that you are in the wrong gendered body can be distressing. It can make it hard for some alters to front and be present in the body. It can also sometimes make alters feel suicidal.

There are some changes systems can make to help them feel less dysphoric, such as:

+ wearing wigs
+ wearing a binder
+ packing
+ growing out body hair
+ shaving body hair
+ having a more masculine haircut or style
+ wearing or buying more feminine/masculine clothes
+ wearing makeup
+ wearing hats and hiding hair
+ getting another alter to front
+ some systems may consider medical transition if it aligns with the needs and wishes of their system.

PART 3

Navigating the World

CHAPTER 18

Studying and Working

Working and Careers

Some people with DID and OSDD are able to work while others are not and that is ok. Living with DID and OSDD is not easy, so if you are not currently working, please do not blame yourselves. Lots of people who live with complex mental health conditions are unable to work. Systems who cannot work or are not currently working may feel ashamed, annoyed or sad. This is completely understandable in a world that has capitalist ideals and values productivity and work. Explaining how you feel to those close to you may help them be more understanding. For example, you could say, 'I would really love to work but I am currently unable to due to my mental health/ DID/OSDD. I am working really hard in therapy so that one day I can hopefully have a job.' Remember that your ability to work does not define your worth or value. All systems are worthy regardless of whether they have a job or not.

Having DID or OSDD does not mean that you will never be able to work. It may just mean that it could be a little harder, your journey may be a little longer, or look a little different. Different alters may want to do different types of work or have very different career aspirations to each other. Deciding on which route to take may be tricky. Some systems may take a vote on it, try out a couple of routes or decide on a role that is best suited for their system as a whole. If you are looking to get into work, you could do some volunteering, work experience, work placements, research and learning (such as short courses) in the areas that you are interested in. Over time, you can build up more contact hours, such as volunteering somewhere local for a couple of hours a week, building up more volunteering, then when you feel ready, applying for a part-time job, and then if it feels possible, a full-time job. Some systems find that working part time, being self-employed or working from home is the best option for them. Through the progression of recovery in therapy and self-work, systems may become more able to work. Just take one step at a time.

Systems often compare themselves to their friends or others their age. They may feel like they are less worthy if they have fewer 'life accomplishments' or are not working. Systems need to remember that people who did not experience childhood trauma have an advantage. People with DID and OSDD had to focus on survival while others did not. Survival is already a massive accomplishment. Objectively, it is more likely that working will be difficult for systems. People with DID and OSDD deal with complex experiences while juggling work, such as switching, amnesia, trauma symptoms and having different alters front. Remember that you are on your own path, life is not a race.

There are also lots of systems out there who have amazing and successful work lives and careers. Unfortunately, there is currently very little representation of this. It is also ok if you are never able to work. There is more to life than work.

OUR EXPERIENCE

We feel sad that our DID and the manifestations of our trauma have got in the way of our life and our career aspirations. We worked so hard at school and got good grades, yet this was not enough. We wonder where we would be in our life had we not had childhood trauma. Recognising that it is not fair and that it is not our fault has helped to shift some of the blame and shame.

We have learned to adapt and have found that being self-employed and running our small business currently works well for us, though we do have other career aspirations. We are hoping that over

time, through recovery in therapy, our journey becomes a little eas-
ier. We grieve the life that we once pictured and hoped for, but we
accept that this is just our reality, and we are making the very best
of it that we can.

Should I Tell My Workplace/School About Having DID/OSDD?

This is entirely up to each system. All work and school environments are different. If you think it would be helpful to let them
know, great. If you do not think it will help, then that is ok too.

It may be helpful to tell your workplace/school/university if
they are able to offer you extra support or understanding. Sometimes other people may notice your different presentations, so you
may decide to disclose that you have a mental health condition/
DID/OSDD. Additionally, some workplaces may require you to
disclose your mental health; however, this is not always the case.

Some systems worry about the stigma attached to DID and
OSDD, so prefer not to say. Workplaces may be more judgemental as
they could be worried about your ability to work and some systems
may choose not to disclose out of fear of losing their job.

Speaking to those close to you about this decision, as well as
other alters, could be helpful. Protectors may be able to help advise
on what they think is best. You may also want to do a pros and
cons list.

Tips for Systems in Education and the Workplace
Telling Others

+ Decide if you want others to know you are a system. Be aware
  that if you tell some people, it may spread to others.

+ Decide if you want to tell a teacher/school nurse/school coun-
  sellor/HR department/occupational health department.

- Will telling others you are a system risk your safety at school or risk you losing your job?

- Are you a covert/overt system? If you are more overt and you are not 'out' and want to remain not out as a system at school/in the workplace then you may want to think about ways to hide your multiplicity, so others do not find out, such as wearing similar clothes.

Organisation

- Think about the best way to organise your time and make sure you can remember everything (for more on tips on system organisation see the section on Coping with Amnesia/ Memory Loss/System Organisation Tips in Chapter 15).

- Do you have one alter who will front most of the time while you are at school/work? Or is it a couple who take turns? Or will you all be present at some point? Will you be ok with the responsibility?

- Know what to do if you switch at school/in the workplace. Have a plan.

- Can you manage the workload? If not, it may be helpful to let someone know this. You do not have to mention you have DID/OSDD if you do not want to, you could just mention you have mental health issues. You may want to consider working less, if possible, such as going from full time to part time to help with the workload. If at school or university, you may want to drop a subject. If at university, you could decide to study part time rather than full time, take a leave of absence or defer your place if you need a break or do not yet feel ready to go.

Extra Help

+ You may wish to enquire if you are eligible for extra time for exams, tests or extensions on work deadlines if this would be helpful. You may also be able to enquire about being in a separate examining room to everyone else.

+ Some schools, colleges or universities may also be able to provide you with extra provisions to help, such as a pen that records lectures to help with memory.

+ Some systems may have more sick days (days of being unwell) than non-systems, due to mental or physical illness. Would it be helpful to let your school/workplace know this?

Look After Yourselves

+ It is important to get plenty of rest and to not over work yourselves. Take time off if you are unwell. Treat yourselves to something nice when you are not working.

CHAPTER 19

Friendships and Relationships

Friendships as a System

For systems, navigating friendships can be a little more complex than the average person, due to their multiplicity. But nevertheless, people with DID and OSDD can be great, kind, understanding and caring friends. All people with DID and OSDD deserve to have supportive friendships. Some systems decide to disclose their DID/OSDD to their friends and others do not. It is up to each system to decide if they would like to do this. It should only happen if the system feels safe and can trust their friends.

It can be helpful for people with DID and OSDD to tell their friends any information they think is important for them to know, such as what DID/OSDD are, some definitions of the key terms, how many alters are in their system, how many alters their friend has already met or what to do if a little fronts. Systems can also point their friend in the direction of helpful educational resources. Some people with DID and OSDD may not always want to share about their system, see no need in sharing details or feel too shy or embarrassed to. This is also ok. Share what you feel comfortable sharing when the time is right for you.

For people with DID and OSDD, if your friends are not respectful and supportive of your mental health or multiplicity and not willing to change or learn, then they may not be the friends for you. If you feel like your friendships are harmful, then you may want to consider finding new friends. It is important that you protect your system. Throughout life, friendships come and go, and that is ok. Using your agency and setting boundaries is important in maintaining healthy friendships.

Some systems may also like to make friends with other systems, as they understand their experience as a multiple, which can be validating.

TIPS FOR SUPPORTING PEOPLE WITH DID AND OSDD

As a non-system, you may not know how to approach navigating a friendship with someone who has DID or OSDD. You may not know much about multiplicity or know how to interact when meeting different alters. Navigate the friendship like you would any other friendship; just be mindful that your system friend may experience some additional challenges. Education and communication are important for both of you.

You may wish to learn about DID/OSDD to better understand their experience. Start with the basics, such as learning about what systems, alters, littles and switches are. It can be reassuring to let your system friend know that you fully accept their multiplicity and will always be there to support them. You could ask if there is anything you can do to help, anything you should know or anything to avoid, such as certain triggers. Over time, you may get to know more of your system friend's different alters and may meet them directly too. Your friend may introduce themselves as different alters and you can simply greet each one as you would a new friend. Some systems may feel shy about opening up and that is ok too. Some people with DID and OSDD have less amnesia between their alters, so when different alters meet you, they may already know or recognise you. If you are ever unsure about something, just ask; open, kind questions can help clarify and strengthen your friendship.

Romantic and Intimate Relationships as a System

Romantic relationships, intimacy, dating, vulnerability and trust can be hard for everyone. However, this can be even harder for DID and OSDD systems.

What Makes It Hard for Systems?

+ **Trauma and triggers** – all systems have experienced childhood trauma. Trauma can cause flashbacks and triggers. Systems may fear being triggered by physical intimacy or fear getting re-traumatised.

+ **Trust** – having experienced childhood trauma and being hurt by someone, systems may find it harder to trust the person they are dating. Or the opposite, they could be too trusting with someone who could be dangerous.

+ **Littles** – having littles (child alters) can be difficult for many reasons, such as the fear of littles fronting during a physically intimate situation or the fear of littles being hurt or getting triggered.

+ **Different tastes** – different alters can have different tastes in romantic partners. In one system there could be some alters who like females only, some alters who like males only, some alters who like all genders and some who are not interested in dating at all. Deciding on who to date can be hard.

+ **Who gets to date?** Deciding who gets to go on dates can be difficult. Some systems only have one alter who is romantically involved with their partner, often the one who fronts most often (the host). However, not all systems have a host.

+ **Fear of abandonment** – some systems may have experienced abandonment and feel scared to date in case this happens

178

again. Abandonment can also include the fear of needs or emotions being abandoned.

+ **Thinking you are undeserving of love** – this can be for a variety of reasons, such as not being cared for or loved as a child, having trauma from family who hurt you, or trauma confusing your view of what love, sex and relationships should be like. Systems may believe that no one would ever love them, which may stop them from even trying to date.

+ **Believing they do not actually like you** – this can stem from trauma or toxic past relationships. Even if someone a system is dating expresses that they like them romantically, alters may find it impossible to believe, even if they want to.

+ **Disclosing your DID/OSDD** – knowing when (or if) to tell the person you are dating that you are a system can be hard and scary. There is still a lot of stigma attached to these conditions and some systems may fear that they will be treated differently or it could be used against them.

Tips for Dating and Romantic Relationships as a System

It is up to each person with DID and OSDD if or when they want to disclose their multiplicity to the person they are dating. It is ok not to tell them straight away. It is also ok if you do not feel comfortable telling them at all. When a relationship becomes more serious or long term it is important for a system to be honest about their DID/OSDD.

Tips for All Systems

+ If you are being physically intimate and a little fronts, *stop* immediately.

◆ If you feel unsafe, scared, get triggered or are not getting good vibes during a date or interaction, remember that you can leave. It is ok to listen to your intuition. Your body and your system's safety is important.

◆ If you go on a first date with someone you have not met before, or have only met a few times and you are worried about safety, tell someone you trust where you are going. You may also want to share your location with friends or family and arrange for a friend to call you if you are feeling uncomfortable, so you have an excuse to leave early.

◆ Let them know that you may have to take things slowly, e.g. with physical intimacy, because of your trauma.

Tips for Disclosure in a Relationship

◆ Explain to them what DID/OSDD are.

◆ Find someone who accepts your multiplicity and respects all of your alters.

◆ Even if they are only dating one of you, they need to accept all of you.

◆ Set clear boundaries and tell your partner who is and who is not dating them.

◆ Talk to them about your system: what being a system is like, what a switch is, mention your triggers (if you trust them) and explain what to do if a little fronts or if you experience a flashback.

◆ If desired, ask them to treat each alter differently as they are like different 'people'.

◆ Make sure that all alters agree that the person you are dating is safe. If it feels scary or unsafe, and is not a trauma memory, stop seeing this person.

◆ Do not feel like you have to disclose details of your trauma to your partner. However, you may choose to share more after some time.

◆ Some systems have polyamorous relationships with another

system or with another non-system. This is where multiple alters are in different relationships with the same person, different alters or the same alter.

Physical Intimacy as a System

Some systems may find physical intimacy and romantic relationships more difficult than non-systems. This could be due to their trauma or due to challenges that come with being a system, such as switching, different alters having different romantic preferences or a history of sexual trauma. A fear of physical intimacy is not your fault and is not a 'bad' thing. If you are not interested or feel scared to engage in intimate situations, that is ok. Physical intimacy may feel scary or uncomfortable as a system. If you or your alters do not feel comfortable in an intimate situation, you can leave. Safety is important, as is being aware of your boundaries. Never do something you do not feel comfortable with. Deciding as a system what you are all comfortable doing, or what certain alters are comfortable doing, and writing this down as a rough set of 'rules', could be helpful. Take things slowly, make sure you are safe, communicate with both your partner and your alters and make sure you trust the person you are with.

Systems or alters may identify as asexual while others may be hypersexual, which can sometimes be a response to trauma. It is valid for systems to choose not to engage in physically intimate relationships and it is equally valid for systems to engage in them, as long as it is safe for everyone, the body is of age and littles are not fronting. Some systems may feel ashamed that they do not have what is viewed as a 'normal' or healthy relationship with physical intimacy. It is possible for a system to heal their relationship with physical intimacy through trauma therapy, safe trusting relationships and honesty and communication with their partner. Some systems do not experience difficulties with physical intimacy and that is perfectly valid too.

Dealing with Non-Romantic Situations Involving Physical Closeness or Intimacy

Some systems may find 'everyday' situations involving intimacy difficult or scary, such as getting a massage, going to yoga, having a haircut, doing close contact sport, going to the dentist or having a medical examination. This can be related to past trauma or feelings of vulnerability.

How to Cope

◆ Bring someone you are close with to these appointments.

◆ Visit these places prior to the appointment to familiarise yourselves with the surroundings.

◆ Bring something comforting with you such as a small soft toy or a grounding pebble.

◆ Focus on your breath.

◆ Tell yourselves you are safe.

◆ Know you can leave if it all gets too much.

◆ Tuck the littles away somewhere safe in the inner world so they are not close to the front.

◆ If you feel comfortable and think it may help, explain to the other person, such as the doctor, that you have DID/OSDD/a mental health condition. Explain that this means this situation may be more difficult for you and ask if they could take things more slowly.

◆ Talk to your therapist or someone you trust on how to deal with this.

◆ Remember that this will not last long.

◆ Buy yourself a treat for getting through it, such as your favourite magazine, a small toy or a new book.

Being a Parent as a System

Whether someone with DID or OSDD decides to have children or not is completely up to them. Being a system does not mean that you cannot have children, it just means you need to be in the right place in your recovery first. Having complex mental health conditions may make being a parent a little harder; however, this does not mean that systems are incapable. Systems can be wonderful parents; their trauma does not prevent this. Experiencing trauma means that people with DID and OSDD are often very empathetic, caring and protective people, which are great traits for a parent to have.

Ideally, a system should have had long-term therapy and be recovered before they have children. A recovered system can have either functional multiplicity or have gone through 'final' fusion, both of which result from long-term work in therapy specifically for DID/OSDD. It is very important for systems to have stability in their life and be in a good place mentally before they have children. It can be very helpful to have a good support system, such as having supportive friends, family and a therapist. Systems should also be able to support their family financially, whether personally or with their partner.

If a system has functional multiplicity, they may want to consider how, when and if they would like to speak to their child about them having DID/OSDD. For some systems, having a child and watching them grow up may occasionally bring up memories of their own childhood trauma. However, for systems who are recovered and have worked through their trauma in therapy, this should not pose any problems. Having children can also be a very healing experience for systems.

It is ok if a system decides that they are not well enough or recovered enough to have children. This can be a hard decision to make and systems may feel anger, sadness or grief about not being able to have a family due to experiencing childhood trauma. This is a brave decision to make. This choice can also be re-evaluated further down the line, if desired and if possible.

Explaining Multiplicity to Children
Multiplicity may seem like a difficult topic to explain to a child. However, there are ways to make it simpler and more age-appropriate.

Both non-systems and systems might choose to explain multiplicity to the children in their life, such as to their own children, nieces or nephews. It is up to each person to decide if or when they would like to tell the children in their life. If the system is more overt, or if the child/children are noticing, it can be helpful to explain multiplicity to them. Some people worry that telling a child could cause them harm and they may want to protect them from this information. However, giving a child an age appropriate explanation can help them to feel more at ease and less confused. If you have a therapist, it can be helpful to plan your explanation with them. You could even rehearse it together through role play. Some people with DID and OSDD decide to teach the child the names of the alters who front most often in their system. However, the child's needs should always come first and sometimes this information can feel like too much for them. Naming alters is usually not recommended for young children and should only be done if you feel it clearly benefits the child. For systems that are more covert, there may be less need to explain multiplicity, as there are fewer or no obvious signs of it. In this case, some people may decide to wait until the child is older, a teenager or an adult.

When explaining multiplicity to a child, it is very important that it remains age appropriate. The older they are, the more information you may decide to give. It is important to keep things simple and avoid scaring young children by revealing too much. It helps to be calm and confident. When explaining DID or OSDD to a young child, you should avoid mentioning the word 'trauma' or give any details that might upset them. Instead, you could just describe what you have, like 'I have different alters who help look after me', 'There are different parts to daddy' or 'Sometimes I switch into different parts of me, like the funny mum or the quiet mum'. With older children or teens, you might gently mention that you went through something difficult or, got hurt as a child, but only if you feel it is appropriate. Always reassure the child that all of your alters love and care about them. It is completely up to you with how much you say, depending on how you think the child will take the information and be able to understand it. Let them know they can ask questions whenever they like and be prepared for their curiosity. It is also helpful to check in with the child afterwards to see how they are feeling. As they grow older you can share more information when it feels appropriate. Once you tell a child, they may also tell others too, like teachers or their friend's parents, so keep this in mind.

There are many ways to explain multiplicity to a child, including:

+ through simple conversations
+ using toys to illustrate the idea
+ drawing pictures together
+ using analogies they can relate to
+ making references to films such as *Inside Out*[1]
+ asking if your therapist could help explain it to them
+ reading a book that helps explain multiplicity.

Books can be helpful for children, (child) alters in a system and supportive adults. For example:

+ The Patchwork Quilt,[2] which uses a quilt to represent different alters
+ My Mommy Has Multiple Parts,[3] which explains DID in a child-friendly way.

Teaching about mental health conditions in schools is also an important way in which the negative stigma can be reduced. Hiding mental health conditions from children can add a sense of mystery, confusion or fear.

Inner System Relationships

Inner system relationships are relationships between different alters in the same system. These relationships can be just as powerful, important and complex as relationships in the real world. For some people, inner system relationships may reflect difficulties with relationships in the outside world, such as not having any friends, having unkind family members or needing more support. Some examples of this are: alters being in romantic relationships with each other, alters having best friends or alters being family, such as siblings, twins, parents, aunts, uncles, children, grandparents, cousins or having a chosen family. Other relationships include professional relationships, neighbours, housemates or other roles of authority or connection like a teacher. Different alters can relate to each other differently. There may be some alters who are closer to other alters. This may be because they have similar trauma, trauma dates, similar interests or are a similar age. Being closer to certain alters means that some alters may know more about them or have more access to their memories.

Not all of the alters in a system will get on or have the same agendas. Some alters may dislike others for various reasons. Some inner system relationships mirror relationships the system has or has had in the outside world, whether traumatic or not. Not everyone in the system will be able to see or communicate with each other in the inner world. Some systems may wish they had more inner system relationships, such as more friendships. It is ok if your system does not have any inner system relationships. Working in therapy and working on system communication can help to develop inner system relationships.

Meeting Other Systems

People with DID and OSDD are not alone in having this mental health condition. There are lots of other systems out there. Reaching out to other people who have similar experiences to you can be meaningful and validating. They *actually* understand and know what it is like to be a system.

Where Can You Meet Other Systems?

There is a DID and OSDD community online and in some places there are also in-person support groups or gatherings of systems.

It is also possible to join a DID/OSDD therapy group in some areas. Systems may decide to meet up with another system that they became friends with online. Be very careful meeting up with people you have met online. You may want to have a video call with them beforehand to help confirm that they are who they say they are. Never meet someone you met online alone for the first time, or at least let someone you trust know where you are going, share your location with them and meet up in a busy public place.

Self-Advocacy

As a system you may sometimes need to be your own advocate, such as in healthcare settings, educational settings or in the workplace. Some people may not believe that you have DID/OSDD, and accessing help, such as therapy, can be hard. It's important to stand up for yourselves. If you are told no, you cannot access help, keep asking, get second opinions and do not give up. If you are in hospital you may need others to advocate for you. Asking friends or family to attend meetings about your care can be helpful as they often know you better than the staff. Some charities also provide free advocacy if you are in hospital, such as if you are sectioned or being told you are not allowed to leave the hospital. Writing notes from meetings you have with others can be a good way to help advocate for your system, as it allows you to remember and reflect upon what was discussed. Voice recording meetings could also be helpful; just remember to ask permission first.

How to Cope with Medical Situations

For people with DID and OSDD, medical situations such as smear tests, medical procedures or surgery can be complex to navigate. Having a plan, recognising your system's needs, checking in with your system and being prepared can help these events go as smoothly as possible.

Some systems find it helpful to write a letter or note to send or give to their doctor/nurse/dentist/surgeon/anaesthetist/medical team etc. You may wish to include:

- your diagnosis and how it manifests; some systems may disclose their multiplicity, while others may instead say they have PTSD or CPTSD (e.g. I have DID which used to be called multiple personality disorder. It is CPTSD caused by childhood trauma. I have different alters who are different ages and genders and have different names and interests. None of us are dangerous or violent. This mental health condition may affect my procedure...)

- how you feel about the event (e.g. I feel very anxious and scared about having this procedure and fear it may be triggering)

- how your multiplicity may affect the event (e.g. Child alters may be present... I may want to run away... I may be too scared to speak... I react to this medication in this way... I may get triggered...)

- what can be done to help (e.g. It would be great if I could bring my friend with me... If my child alters are around, please could you... I would appreciate it if a female member of staff could... I may need...)

- a closing sentence to thank them (e.g. I am sure that with clear communication we can work through this together to guarantee a successful outcome. I greatly appreciate you reading these notes and thank you and your team for being patient and understanding. Do let me know if you have any questions or would like any more information).

PART 4

Systems in Society and the Media

CHAPTER 20

Representation and Visibility

Multiplicity in the Media

The media has depicted multiplicity in a variety of ways, through both fictional portrayals and real-life experiences. At the time of writing, the author is unaware of any representations specifically depicting OSDD; however, many experiences of DID are applicable and relatable to people with OSDD-1. Real presentations of multiplicity can be seen in documentaries, autobiographies, podcasts and social media posts such as YouTube videos. Fictional depictions of multiplicity can be seen in novels, comic books, films, theatre and television shows. Many fictional representations of DID are sensationalised and some portray people with this disorder as monsters, criminals or as having evil alters. The most famous example is the film *Split*, which has been widely criticised for its stigmatising depiction of DID.[1] It is important that people recognise that many of these fictional portrayals are inaccurate, damaging and only perpetuate the stigma and continue to spread misinformation. The DID and OSDD online community have raised many issues with the inaccurate fictional portrayals.

An article in the *European Journal of Trauma & Dissociation* found that 'inaccurate, stigmatizing media depictions of DID perpetuate misconceptions about DID and contribute to delays in seeking treatment and getting accurately diagnosed, and increased shame and self-loathing among individuals with DID'.[2] There are real life consequences to these inaccurate portrayals. Representations of real cases are a much better source of accuracy. People with DID and OSDD may want to avoid watching inaccurate representations as they can be invalidating, hurtful or triggering. Systems deserve to have more accurate representations in all forms of media.

Some examples of accurate presentations of multiplicity in the media include:

♦ Dissociative Identity Disorder Documentary: *The Lives I Lead*[3]

♦ *The Woman With 15 Personalities*[4] (documentary)

♦ *Petals of a Rose* (short film)[5]

♦ *Multiple Personality Disorder: The Search for Deadly Memories.*[6] (Content warning: Please note that this documentary follows three DID systems and the first system is pressured to remember trauma. The author of this book does not condone this.)

♦ *Inside Out.*[7] Many systems find this film a helpful way to explain multiplicity even though it is not specifically about different alters.

♦ *Severance.*[8] Although this television series is not about people with DID or OSDD, its concept explores multiplicity. The characters have two distinct selves, a work self and a personal self, that function similarly to alters. These selves have different identities and personalities and experience amnesia between each other. The show also uses terms like 'integration' and 'switch' which are commonly associated with DID and OSDD.

♦ There are more recommendations in the Recommended Resources section at the end of this book, which includes podcasts, fiction and non-fiction books.

TIPS FOR SUPPORTING PEOPLE WITH DID AND OSDD
Try not to speak about inaccurate portrayals of multiplicity, like the film *Split*, or compare systems to inaccurate portrayals.

Well-Known Systems

Unfortunately, there are not many system role models or examples of famous people who have DID. At the time of writing, the author does not know of any who have OSDD. This is most probably because OSDD is a newer diagnosis (2013) compared to DID and MPD. Both DID and OSDD systems can benefit from having role models to look up to, in the same way people without DID and OSDD do. It can be helpful for systems to see examples of other systems living happy, functional and successful lives. Without these examples, the future as a system may seem daunting or unknown.

Some well-known DID systems include:

♦ **AnnaLynne McCord**, an actress, known for her role in *90210*, model and activist who was diagnosed with DID.[9]

♦ **Dissociadid**, a YouTube channel run by a system which documents their experiences with DID.[10]

♦ **The Entropy System**, a YouTube channel run by a system which documents their experiences with DID.[11]

♦ **Herschel Walker**, a former American football player; he wrote the book *Breaking Free: My Life with Dissociative Identity Disorder.*[12]

♦ **Jess from MultiplicityAndMe**, who was previously diagnosed with DID and posted videos about her experience with DID on her YouTube channel 'Multiplicity and Me'. Her system has since integrated and gone through 'final' fusion.[13]

♦ **Joan Baez**, a singer and songwriter, who has publicly shared that she has DID. She discusses her mental health in the documentary *Joan Baez: I Am a Noise.*[14]

♦ **Karen Overhill**, the focus of the book *Switching Time*, a book written by her psychiatrist Richard Baer about her multiple personality disorder, now known as DID.[15]

♦ **Kim Noble**, an artist and author with DID.[16]

♦ **Truddi Chase** was diagnosed with multiple personality disorder, now known as DID. Her system wrote their autobiography *When Rabbit Howls*, which became a *New York Times* bestseller.[17]

(We do not endorse or agree with everything that these systems have produced; this is just a list of some well-known systems. There are also well-known systems that do not live in English speaking countries.)

The General Public
Stigma

For many systems, managing the symptoms of DID and OSDD is only part of the struggle, they must also contend with the stigma attached to their conditions. The stigma can result in people not believing them, which in some cases can be life threatening. Things need to change. People need to learn the reality: that systems are not criminals or dangerous, they are just people who experienced trauma as a child and deserve love and kindness. Widespread (re) education can help reduce the stigma and rewrite the narratives, thus creating space for systems to be honest and open about their experiences and to help them to access the help that they need.

How to Reduce Stigma

The stigma can be reduced by changing the narrative. This can be done by bringing up up dissociative disorders in conversations with people you know and speaking to your work colleagues/family/friends about multiplicity. Have they heard of DID or OSDD? If not, explain it to them and have an open conversation.

The stigma can also be reduced through education. Educate yourself in as many ways possible, such as reading books on DID and OSDD, learning from other systems and watching documentaries. (See Recommended Resources at the back of the book.) Encourage others to do the same. Having more accurate representations of DID and OSDD in the media can also help to reduce the stigma.

Fakeclaiming

Fakeclaiming is when other people claim or assume that a DID or OSDD system is faking being a system. Assumptions like this are very damaging. Fakeclaiming mostly exists online, with forums and web pages dedicated to fakeclaiming systems. It is not up to someone from the general public to 'decide' if a system is faking or not. The only people who can do this are trained mental health professionals such as psychiatrists and psychotherapists who specialise in trauma. If you think a system is faking, keep it to yourself. Denying a system's experience and identity can be harmful. It is discrimination and may come from a place of misunderstanding, ignorance, insecurity or sometimes hate. The vast majority of systems are not faking.

What to Do If You Have Been Fakeclaimed

If you have been fakeclaimed, remember that no one knows your system better than you do. If you experience fakeclaiming online, block the account(s) and delete the comment(s). If it happens in real life, if possible try to distance yourselves from this person as much as you can. If it happens in school or the workplace, you may wish to report this person. If you would like to and feel safe doing so, you could point the fakeclaimer to a source of information or try to educate them on DID and OSDD. However, you have no obligation and it is not your responsibility to educate others. Unfortunately, many fakeclaimers are unwilling to learn. You should prioritise keeping your system safe. Being fakeclaimed may cause you to doubt yourselves; if so, read the tips on How to Help with System Doubt in Chapter 8.

TIPS FOR SUPPORTING PEOPLE WITH DID AND OSDD
Never fakeclaim a system or doubt their experiences. Instead, listen to them, validate their experiences and support them.

Are Mental Illnesses Trendy?

Some people think that others fake mental illnesses because they are 'cool' or are currently 'in trend'. This is a damaging belief. Almost all people who live with a mental illness are *not* faking it. Mental illnesses are not desirable and they are not cool. They make life *more* difficult and complex. They are not fun to deal with. A minuscule amount of people may be faking a mental illness because they think it is cool or because they want attention. This is a separate and serious issue which these people need help with. It should *always* be assumed that if someone shares that they have a mental health condition or mental illness, they are telling the truth. Telling someone they are making it up, attention seeking or pretending is *not* ok. It can feel very invalidating and make the person's mental health deteriorate even further. The only people who should tell someone that they do not have a mental illness are mental health professionals, after an assessment for a diagnosis. However, it is important to note that even mental health professionals can be biased, misdiagnose and be uneducated in particular fields. Getting second opinions can help with this. Some people may *want* a mental illness because they think it is cool. This is also not ok. Romanticising mental illnesses is equally as damaging. It focuses on all the 'interesting' aspects of a disorder and leaves out all the difficulties.

The System Community

The system community is most active online, where systems can connect, share, advocate and find support. These spaces can help systems feel less alone and more understood. Some systems like to share anonymously online, others prefer to follow accounts that speak about multiplicity.

You can find system communities on platforms such as Instagram, Facebook, YouTube, TikTok, Reddit, Tumblr, Quora, Discord and in online support groups. If you are unsure of how to find these communities you could try searching hashtags, such as #didsystem, #osddsystem and #dissociativeidentitydisorder. Be aware that some posts or conversations may be triggering, so be careful. In some areas, there are also in-person options, such as support groups, therapy groups or events, like conferences. It is important to be mindful of what you share, both online and offline, to keep your system safe. You may want to avoid sharing details about your child alters, trauma and personal information. The system community can be a validating and supportive space to connect with others who truly understand.

Trigger Warnings

When speaking about difficult topics online, such as on social media, people sometimes put a trigger warning before the information.

They may also list the content warning in a few words and substitute some of the letters with a star icon, so that the words themselves are less triggering. Even if you do not find the content triggering, other people might, so it is important to put a warning. Trigger warnings are abbreviated as TW. Here is an example: *TW s*lf-h*rm*, standing for self-harm. Many academic books or memoirs about mental health do not include trigger warnings, so approach with caution, read one page at a time and check in with your system to see how everyone feels.

System Pride Day

System pride day occurs every year on 23 February. It is a day to celebrate DID, OSDD, P-DID and UDD systems. There is also a system pride flag. Systems may not feel proud that they are a system, but instead feel proud *of* their system. System pride day is separate from LGBTQ+ pride, although some systems may still identify as LGBTQ+. System pride is not specifically about sexuality, attraction or gender. Instead, system pride is about being proud of your system and of other systems. There is also a DID Awareness Day that takes place on 5 March every year. At the time of writing there are not any OSDD, P-DID or UDD awareness days that the author is aware of.

> **OUR EXPERIENCE**
> *Joining the system community on Instagram has been amazing for our system. It is so validating to hear about other systems whose experiences are similar to our own; this helps us to feel less alone in our experiences. We are so grateful to be able to connect with other systems worldwide through this community.*

Advocacy

Some people, both systems and non-systems, may wish to do advocacy work to help spread education and awareness of DID and OSDD; this is great. People can advocate in many different ways, such as on social media, distributing information leaflets, or in the community, such as by giving talks about DID and OSDD in schools, community centres or places of worship. People can also join charities, groups and organisations to volunteer in advocacy efforts, such as signing petitions, going on peaceful protests, assisting with training and supporting fundraisers. Some people become healthcare, legal, victim or peer advocates for people who have experienced trauma. Other people focus on changing mental health related laws or policies. Educating your friends and family is also a great way to help spread awareness and to help demystify DID and OSDD.

PART 5

Getting Help

CHAPTER 21

Assessment and Diagnosis

How to Get an Assessment and Possible Diagnosis

If you are an undiagnosed system, know that you are just as valid as those who have a diagnosis. For some systems, getting a diagnosis may feel very important, and in some countries, a diagnosis may be required in order to access specific therapy. However, in other countries or locations, a diagnosis may not be needed in order to receive therapy for DID or OSDD. A DID or OSDD diagnosis should always be given by a qualified clinician.

In the UK

+ **Through the National Health Service (NHS)** – Unfortunately it can be difficult to get an assessment for dissociative disorders through the NHS, as few NHS trusts offer them. However, it is always worth asking and it may require some persistence. If you are under a community mental health team or have a care coordinator you could ask them. If not, you could ask your GP. In some cases, you may be given a diagnosis by a psychiatrist. If your local NHS trust does not offer an assessment, there is also the charity Clinic for Dissociative Studies (CDS)[1] which offers assessments and therapy in various locations across England and accepts referrals from the NHS. All options may have long waiting lists.

- **Privately** – There are a few places in the UK that offer private assessments, such as Beacon House,[2] The Pottergate Centre[3] and The Complex Trauma And Dissociation Clinic (CTAD Clinic).[4]

    Private assessments for dissociative disorders are expensive. Check out all the organisations that offer private assessments as their prices may vary. It may also be possible to get an assessment from someone who is still training, which may reduce the cost.

Unfortunately (at the time of writing) there is currently more help for systems in the private sector as the NHS is behind when it comes to offering assessment and therapy for DID and OSDD.

Assessment and Diagnosis in the Rest of the World

Depending on where you live, the route to an assessment for DID/OSDD may vary. You may be able to get diagnosed by a therapist, psychiatrist, psychotraumatologist or psychologist, all of whom may be trained in giving assessments or may specialise in dissociative disorders. You could try researching the route online or ask your GP/primary healthcare provider, mental health team or therapist.

For some systems, the country they live in may not offer assessments for dissociative disorders or the DID and OSDD diagnoses may not exist. If possible, systems may decide to travel to a nearby country that offers assessments or they may be able to have an online assessment with a trained professional who lives abroad. Systems may also be able to get online therapy from a therapist who lives abroad. In some countries DID and OSDD may still be referred to as MPD (multiple personality disorder).

Mental health systems vary between countries. However, most mental health systems are not perfect, especially for people with DID and OSDD. Access to help varies between countries. Access to mental health support for systems is also a socio-political and economic issue.

Assessment (and Diagnostic Instruments and Dissociation Screening Tools)

The most common assessment for dissociative disorders starts with two screening instruments: the Dissociative Experiences Scale (DES-II)[5] and the Somatoform Dissociation Questionnaire (SDQ-5/SDQ-20).[6] These can be found on the ISSTD website.[7] You may find it helpful to look at one of the dissociation screening questionnaires to see if it would be helpful for you to seek a professional assessment for dissociative disorders. The Multidimensional Inventory of Dissociation (MID)[8] and the Dissociative Disorders Interview Schedule (DDIS)[9] can both be viewed online. The full assessment can only be carried out by a trained mental health professional. It is done in interview form and takes several hours. The recommended assessment is the Structured Clinical Interview for DSM-5 Dissociative Disorders (SCID-D).[10]

Diagnostic Manuals: The DSM-5 and the ICD-11

The Diagnostic and Statistical Manual of Mental Disorders (DSM) and International Classification of Diseases (ICD) are the diagnostic manuals used to diagnose mental health conditions, including dissociative disorders. Generally the UK and Europe follow the ICD and the United States follows the DSM. However, private assessments in the UK may use the DSM. At the time of writing, the most up-to-date editions are the DSM-5 and the ICD-11. The DSM-5 includes the diagnoses DID and OSDD. The ICD-11 includes the diagnoses DID and P-DID.

Misdiagnosis

Unfortunately, it is common for systems to receive misdiagnoses. This is due to many factors, such as stigma and the lack of education and training that mental health professionals receive on DID and OSDD. Some systems can remain misdiagnosed for many years and still be waiting for a DID or OSDD diagnosis. Systems can also receive multiple misdiagnoses. This does not make them any less valid. Being misdiagnosed can be invalidating, upsetting and may stop systems from receiving the treatment (therapy) that they need. Loewenstein states that, 'across studies, DID patients spend an average of 5–12.4 years in the mental health system before correct diagnosis'.[11] Reinders and Veltman state that 'from the moment of seeking treatment for symptoms to the time of an accurate diagnosis of DID, individuals receive an average of four prior other diagnoses, inadequate pharmacological treatment, have several hospital admissions and consequently spend many years in mental health services'.[12] They recognise that 'years of misdirected treatment result in protracted personal suffering'.[13] Misdiagnoses are not the fault of the individual but the medical systems in which they reside. Reinders and Veltman outline some causes of DID misdiagnosis that include 'insufficient training in recognising trauma related dissociation, limited exposure to accurate scientific information about DID, unfamiliarity with the spectrum of dissociative disorders, symptom similarities with other disorders and the aetiology debate'.[14] The lack of acceptance and understanding of DID and OSDD amongst professionals can greatly complicate and elongate a system's recovery journey. Hopefully, over time, these high rates of misdiagnosis will begin to decrease.

Common Misdiagnoses

+ Asperger syndrome
+ Attention deficit hyperactivity disorder (ADHD)
+ Bipolar disorder
+ Clinical depression
+ Cyclothymia
+ Generalised anxiety disorder
+ Obsessive compulsive disorder (OCD)
+ Panic disorder
+ Personality disorders (such as borderline personality disorder (BPD), histrionic personality disorder and dependent personality disorder)

- Psychosis
- Schizophrenia

OUR EXPERIENCE

We were misdiagnosed with BPD. This seems quite a common misdiagnosis amongst systems. We had dialectical behaviour therapy (DBT) for our (misdiagnosed) BPD but found it difficult to remember all the skills. We now know this was due to our amnesia. Our group therapists would often tell us we were dissociating during the group sessions, yet we were unaware of this. We were told we should get an assessment for dissociative disorders, so we did. We were then diagnosed with DID. We are grateful that our DBT therapists noticed us dissociating and listened to us when we told them about our different alters, whom at that time we referred to as 'personas'.

Undiagnosed Systems
Diagnosis and Validity

People should be wary of self-diagnosing DID and OSDD; however, equally, not all systems are able to access an assessment or diagnosis. Having a diagnosis does not change your experience as a multiple. Some undiagnosed systems may feel less valid without a diagnosis, while others may not feel the need for a diagnosis.

All systems are different and will have different reasons as to why they are undiagnosed. It is important to show the same respect and kindness to both diagnosed and undiagnosed systems. Remember that all people diagnosed with DID and OSDD were once undiagnosed. Systems do not owe you any reasons as to why they are undiagnosed. A diagnosis is a privilege that is not accessible to all.

Reasons for remaining undiagnosed include:

- the high cost of an assessment
- not being able to access the services that provide assessments or there not being any
- not being 'out' as a system

+ feeling scared to have an assessment, such as fearing it could result in losing your job
+ the stigma
+ it not being safe to, such as having medical trauma or still living with abusers
+ being too young to get a diagnosis
+ not wanting to believe that you are a system.

How Do You Choose to Understand Your Diagnosis?

Some systems and mental health professionals do not agree with calling DID and OSDD a 'disorder' as they feel this insinuates that something is wrong. This author agrees. Referring to systems as being mentally *ill* or mentally *unwell* suggests that systems are not well when there is actually nothing 'wrong' with them. Developing DID and OSDD is a response to trauma, it is the brain's clever coping mechanism, a helpful adaptation; there is nothing wrong about this. The adaptation allows systems to become *more* 'well', allowing them to survive and get on with everyday life. Calling DID and OSDD a disorder or illness is comparing brains. It assumes that neurotypicals' brains are 'well' and 'normal' while systems' brains are 'unwell' and 'not normal'. Neurodiverse brains are not 'unwell', just different. Systems' brains should be celebrated for being clever, adaptive and special; different, yes, but not 'unwell'. 'Unwell' suggests that systems need to become 'well' again, but their brains developed differently as a child in the first place, due to trauma, so there is no 'well' to return to. Having one binary of 'well' or 'normal' people is selective and discriminatory. People can replace the word 'disorder' for the word 'condition' if they would like to. It is fine if systems consider their DID/OSDD a disorder or a mental illness and it is fine if they do not. Each system's preference should be respected.

Beyond the Medical Gaze

There are several gazes in which DID and OSDD can be viewed. The most common is the medical gaze. Society and the healthcare system perceive mental health conditions through the medical and scientific gaze. By only considering multiplicity through the medical gaze, one is denying its entirety. The whole picture is not acknowledged.

An alternative gaze is the philosophical gaze, which argues that one cannot give an unbiased specification of mental illness and that the idea of mental illness should be changed to represent people's diversity of cognition, rather than seeing 'non-normal' people as other or unwell.

The pathologising of mental illnesses can be damaging. Pathologising DID and OSDD can shift the blame onto systems, deny a system's existence through misdiagnosis, offer unhelpful psychiatric medication and cause more trauma through psychiatric hospitalisations. People with DID and OSDD are more than their 'symptoms'.

Disabled?

Are DID and OSDD systems disabled? Some people consider people with DID and OSDD to be disabled and some do not. Either view is valid. It is up to each system to decide if they consider themselves disabled as a system. All choices should be respected.

The UK government states, 'You're disabled under the Equality Act 2010 if you have a physical or mental impairment that has a "substantial" and "long-term" negative effect on your ability to do normal daily activities.'[15] For many systems this may be the case.

In some countries being classed as disabled, due to multiplicity, may help systems access monetary government assistance or benefits. For some systems this is important as their multiplicity may affect their ability to work or look after themselves. If you think this could be helpful for your system or a system you know, then research this online or seek advice or support.

CHAPTER 22

Recovery and Therapy

What Does Recovery Look Like?
(Recovery Through Therapy)

In the article 'Treatment of dissociative identity disorder: Leveraging neurobiology to optimize success' it states that 'a rich literature of case histories, clinical examples, and empirical work affirm that DID is treatable' and 'the evidence demonstrates that carefully staged trauma-focused psychotherapy for DID results in improvement'.[1] The same goes for OSDD.

The Three Phases of Recovery/Treatment

There is a phase-oriented treatment model for DID and OSDD systems that some therapists follow, as mentioned by the International Society for the Study of Trauma and Dissociation.[2] The phases are:

+ **Phase 1:** Establishing Safety, Stabilisation and Symptom Reduction

+ **Phase 2:** Confronting, Working Through and Integrating Traumatic Memories

+ **Phase 3:** Integration and Rehabilitation. Systems may decide on functional multiplicity or 'final' fusion.

Other types of therapy such as the Internal Family Systems (IFS) Model follow a vertical model rather than a phased model, where the phases happen simultaneously.

Integration

Integration is a process that often happens naturally through therapy where the dissociative walls between alters are reduced. This allows alters to come closer together, share more memories and work together more effectively. Integration is not the same as 'final' fusion. Instead, it is an ongoing process of connection and cooperation that allows for more agency and functionality in a system's everyday life.

'Final' Fusion and Functional Multiplicity

There are two main routes that can be taken in recovery, through therapy, and it is up to each system to decide which route they would like to take. Both recovery paths are valid and can lead to healing. There is no right or wrong choice. It is also ok to not know which route you would like to take and some systems may just see where therapy naturally takes them over time. The idea of your system changing may seem scary and that is ok. There is no rush to make any decision.

'Final' fusion

'Final' fusion is a process in which all alters in a system fully merge into one unified identity. This single self holds the experiences, memories and qualities of everyone in the system. 'Final' fusion usually takes many years, so it is not an instant change, it happens slowly. 'Final' fusion can only happen through therapy and all alters must agree to it for it to happen. Some systems who have gone through 'final' fusion may no longer identify as having DID.

Some systems prefer this option as it reduces dissociative symptoms and reduces the difficulties that being multiple can bring. Having no switches may make life easier, such as making it easier to hold down a job. Some systems are afraid of 'losing' their alters with 'final' fusion. Although it may seem this way, this is not what happens. Instead, it is more of an integration, where the alters all come together to become one. The alters do not disappear or die, they will always be there whether 'final' fusion happens or not. It will just be less obvious with 'final' fusion. The integration results in a new personality that has parts of all the alters.

Other systems may feel that 'final' fusion is the recovery path that is right for them. 'Final' fusion is not always final, the person may split again and old alters may return, or new alters may be created. For example, this could happen after a new traumatic experience.

Functional multiplicity

Functional multiplicity is deciding to continue to live life as a system, in a way that allows full functionality in everyday life. The alters remain separate and distinct but they cooperate to create harmony within the system. This route also requires therapy to help stabilise alters and requires trauma work for all the alters who hold trauma. Alters may become closer through therapy, with memory integration and some alters may fuse, yet a system of alters still remains. System communication is important with functional multiplicity.

This is the preferred route for a lot of systems. Some systems decide to stay multiple because they have lived as a system for most of their life and see no reason or have no desire to change this. Systems may feel that they do not want to 'lose' the other alters as they are. Alters may wish to remain their separate selves. Even though the alters do not die with 'final' fusion, it may feel like this for the system. It may feel like they are losing parts of themselves that they have come to know and love. It may feel like losing a whole family and the idea of 'final' fusion may seem lonely.

How to Decide?

Both recovery routes are valid and it is a choice you must discuss with everyone in your system. It needs to be a system decision, not an individual one. Having each alter vote on their preferred recovery destination allows you to find out everyone's preference. Some therapists may 'forcefully' direct systems down the path of 'final' fusion. This is not ethical. It is up to each system to decide on their own recovery destination. If your therapist is adamant that you must have 'final' fusion and you want functional multiplicity, tell them. If they will not work with you towards functional multiplicity then it may be best to find a new therapist who will.

There is no rush for systems to decide which recovery route to take. Systems also do not have to decide. Instead they may see which route their system naturally takes through therapy and recovery.

OUR EXPERIENCE

We used to fear 'final' fusion. We think it was a fear of the unknown. We have now experienced what it is like to unburden trauma, integrate memories and have alters fuse. This healing has been beautiful. Now we no longer fear the coming together of our alters. For us, we think that 'final' fusion could make our life a lot easier; however, we are still a little hesitant to this idea. We currently have no agenda as to which recovery route we will take, we are just seeing what naturally happens through therapy. Our only priority is helping our littles to feel safe, unburdened from trauma and not stuck in the past.

All About Therapy

Therapy is how systems heal from trauma. Sadly, not all therapists understand multiplicity, so finding one who does may take a little longer. However, there are excellent therapists out there who understand multiplicity and are very supportive of systems. If you can access therapy, it is always a good idea. You can take things as slowly as you like in therapy. There is no rush to speak about difficult topics if your system is not ready. Therapy for DID and OSDD is likely to last a while. It varies for each system, but it may take around a couple of years to ten years, due to the complexity of these conditions. Therapy is not easy and is not a quick fix. It requires a lot of work. However, the work pays off as systems become unburdened from their trauma and gain a more functional and fulfilling life.

What Type of Therapy?

Specialised, long-term, trauma-informed psychotherapy, also known as talking therapy, is the recommended therapy for DID and OSDD as it allows systems to recover and heal. It is important to find a therapist who has had relevant training and experience working with dissociative disorders, ideally DID and OSDD, and complex trauma. However, for some, finding a specialised therapist may be difficult. If you cannot find a specialised therapist in your area you could try online therapy. Or alternatively, have general talking therapy or a different type of therapy, while you continue looking for a therapist who has worked with DID/OSDD.

Other types of therapy that may be helpful in addition to talking therapy include:

+ art psychotherapy
+ music psychotherapy
+ play psychotherapy
+ dance and movement psychotherapy
+ psychodynamic therapy
+ family therapy
+ drama psychotherapy
+ sensorimotor psychotherapy
+ somatic psychotherapy
+ animal-assisted therapy
+ Internal Family Systems (IFS, if the therapist is experienced with DID)
+ eye movement desensitisation and reprocessing (EMDR, if the therapist is experienced with DID)
+ dialectical behavioural therapy (DBT) and cognitive behavioural therapy (CBT).

Some therapists may use multiple therapy modalities or approaches within their sessions.

Hypnosis was used in the past as a treatment for people with

DID and OSDD and is still occasionally used today. Hypnosis is controversial as it can take agency and control away from systems, which can be triggering and make them feel powerless. Hypnosis should never be used to try to force or retrieve memories in systems. This can be harmful and retraumatising. Many therapists and systems feel that trauma memories should be remembered naturally, in a system's own time. It is up to each system to decide if hypnosis is for them.

Alternative therapies, such as art therapy, can help in different ways to talking therapy. They can help access the subconscious, help alters who are unable to speak about their trauma, and help alters to feel safer in the body as trauma is stored in the body as well as the mind. Alternative forms of therapy can also be more helpful for some alters, such as littles and non-speaking alters. Using alternative methods to explore trauma which do not involve talking may feel safer.

Talking therapy should be a system's first priority. If a system can also access alternative therapy it can be a helpful addition but it is not essential. If a system is unable to access talking therapy but able to access an alternative therapy and they think it will help, they can try it.

The commitment to therapy, especially if you attend more than once a week, may impact other areas of a system's life such as work and socialising.

Group Therapy

Group therapy specifically for DID and OSDD can be helpful for some systems. For some it is the only available option. Group therapy may be a helpful way to learn about and learn from other systems. However, it can also be triggering for some systems, for example if they are asked to speak about their trauma or listen to others speak about their trauma. In terms of long-term recovery, individual therapy is needed. Group therapy can be an addition to individual therapy, if desired.

Where to Access Therapy

In the UK you can receive therapy through the NHS or privately. In the NHS there may be long waiting lists or no appropriate services for DID/OSDD in your area. However, it is still worth enquiring about. Speak to your GP or, if relevant, your community mental health team about accessing therapy.

You may be able to access other types of therapy on the NHS more easily, such as trauma therapy, which is not specifically for systems. These therapists may not understand DID or OSDD. However, some may be willing to learn more about these conditions so that they can try and help. It is up to you to decide if you think this could be helpful. Systems in the UK can also speak to their GP about applying for funding to access therapy provided by other organisations, such as Beacon House, The CTAD Clinic and the CDS. In other parts of the world, systems may be able to find support through national mental health organisations, private trauma specialists or contact plural or trauma non-profits for further information.

Some therapists and counsellors only work online and use a live video streaming platform for their sessions, meaning that you do therapy from your home. Other therapists meet with their clients in person, such as in their office, in their home, in an organisation or in a hospital outpatient department. There are pros and cons to both types of therapy and different systems have different preferences.

OUR EXPERIENCE

We are very privileged and extremely grateful to be in therapy for our DID. Being in the right therapy with a therapist who understands trauma and multiplicity has helped us so much. Finally everyone in our system feels seen and heard. This is so important because so many of us have been 'hidden' for so long. We know that we will be in therapy for a while and at times this can feel overwhelming, but we know that it is the only way forward! Therapy is hard work and after some therapy sessions we can feel exhausted and unable to do anything else. We make sure to take things easy and be extra kind to ourselves. Occasionally, it can feel like we are getting worse before we are getting better, as therapy brings up difficult memories and emotions. However, we know that we are making progress and have come such a long way already.

With our system, our therapist does Internal Family Systems therapy with an awareness of attachment and trauma-informed approaches. We also do some somatic work and sensorimotor psychotherapy. Our therapist understands social and family dynamics, responses to trauma and has experience helping other clients with DID, OSDD and CPTSD. Additionally, we have had art therapy in the past which was also so helpful for our system, in a different way to talking therapy.

Cost of Therapy

Unfortunately, it can be difficult to access free therapy for DID and OSDD. In the UK, you may be lucky enough to access it, but it is mostly a postcode lottery. If you are not offered specialist therapy, you may be able to get other therapy on the NHS, which is free. In the United States some people may have an insurance plan that covers therapy. In the rest of the world, therapy may be available through public health services, insurance plans or by paying privately.

If you are waiting for free therapy or cannot afford private therapy, there are other options. Some organisations, charities, counsellors and private therapists offer a sliding scale, offer reductions to the cost of therapy, offer low-cost therapy or do work pro bono. This is usually for people who are not working, are receiving government benefits/welfare or are on a low income. Therapists or counsellors who are still training also often offer reduced rates. If you are in the UK and you receive a Personal Independent Payment (PIP), your GP's social prescriber may be able to help you apply for help to cover the costs of private therapy.

Counselling is another option to get support and can be more affordable; however, it is not the same as psychotherapy. You may be able to receive counselling at your school, university or workplace for free. Some workplaces have private health insurance, which could help you get therapy at a lower cost. If you can afford it, there is also private therapy. Prices per session will vary. Private therapy can be a significant financial burden. However, therapy for DID and OSDD is an important investment in healing, improved functionality and overall wellbeing.

Finding a Therapist

If possible, choose a therapist who understands, has experience with and has been trained in working with complex trauma and DID/OSDD. The ISSTD, Multiplied by One Org and Psychology Today all have online therapist directories. In the UK, you can use the therapist directory on the British Association for Counselling and Psychotherapy (BACP) website, or the UK Council for Psychotherapy (UKCP) website, to ensure your therapist is trained. Other online therapist finders can also be used. These may have the option to specify certain mental health conditions or search using keywords. If it is not possible to select or include DID and OSDD, other keywords you could try searching include 'dissociation', 'dissociative disorders', 'trauma' or 'CPTSD'. See the Recommended Resources for more information.

Telling Your Therapist You Are a System

Some people with DID and OSDD may be in therapy but not yet have told their therapist that they are a system. It may feel daunting; however, it is important that you tell your therapist so that you get the appropriate help. The sooner you tell your therapist the sooner you will get help for your multiplicity. When/if you tell your therapist, it can be helpful to have a list of all the reasons, examples and evidence that you are a system. Unfortunately, some therapists may not believe you or not believe that DID and OSDD exist. If this is the case, if possible you may wish to find a new therapist who does believe you and who understands multiplicity.

Therapy Red Flags

Most therapists and counsellors are professional; however, occasionally some issues may occur in therapy. If these issues arise it may be helpful to bring them up with your therapist to try and resolve them, if you feel comfortable doing so and it is safe to. It may make you reconsider whether it is healthy or helpful to continue working with your therapist. If things are not working between you and your therapist, it is ok to stop and to find another. Your therapist might not be the right fit for you, and that is ok. Below are some red flags to look out for in therapy.

Therapy and Multiplicity

+ Therapists who force switches.
+ Therapists who outwardly favour some alters over others.
+ Therapists who only want to speak to the system's host.
+ Therapists who force a certain recovery destination on you (such as 'final' fusion).
+ Therapists who are dismissive of your alters, do not believe you have them, or do not believe you have DID/OSDD.

Therapists' Views and Behaviours

+ Therapists who get angry at you.
+ Therapists who are racist/sexist/homophobic/discriminatory.
+ Therapists who flirt with you or touch you without your consent.

Therapy and Trauma

+ Therapists who share alters' secrets.
+ Therapists who make your recovery feel rushed.
+ Therapists who do not understand dissociation or trauma.
+ Therapists who make you disclose details of your trauma or force or encourage you to remember traumatic memories when you are not ready to.

Professionalism

* Therapists who do not keep your information confidential. However, there is an exception if they think that you are in danger to yourselves and they may contact your emergency contact.
* Therapists who do not belong to a registered governing body organisation or do not have the sufficient training.
* Therapists who repeatedly cancel your session at the last minute or change your session time a lot.
* Therapists who give instructions as to what medication you should take (they are not qualified to give these instructions, unless they are also your psychiatrist).

There are also other red flags which may come up in therapy. If something does not feel right, maybe it is not. Bring it up with your therapist or speak to someone you trust and ask for their opinion or advice. It is very important for the therapeutic relationship to feel safe and be safe.

'Recovery'

Some people think that the term recover is not appropriate when speaking about DID and OSDD. Recover means to get better, so to recover from DID and OSDD suggests that being multiple is not well or not good. Recovering suggests going back to how you were before. Systems cannot return to a 'normal' previous state of health because they never had one, due to childhood trauma. Their brains adapted to trauma and developed differently. It is important that everyone knows that there is nothing wrong with systems. When systems speak of recovery they refer to recovering from the effects of trauma, not erasing their multiplicity. Being a non-system is not the only way or the right way to exist, although this may be what some systems want.

Systems can recover in the sense that they can get better, but this is not by returning to how they were before. It is instead about creating a better life through support and therapy, learning to live with their alters. It is more of a discovery rather than recovery. To 'recover' is to be free from the manifestations of trauma, to live a life that is not dictated by trauma.

Some DID and OSDD systems may say that they have recovered and therefore no longer need or want the DID/OSDD diagnosis. Some people will say that even if they have gone through 'final' fusion, they will still always have DID/OSDD. Some systems may not mind the term recover, whereas others may not feel like it fits. Some people with DID and OSDD may prefer other terms, such as *healing*. It is up to each individual system to decide how they feel about this term and what it means to them. This decision should be respected.

Will We Ever Recover?

Some people have expectations for a system to 'fully' recover or recover by a certain time. This can cause systems to feel shame if their recovery is taking longer than they hoped or longer than they feel others expect.

It is important for non-systems to know how much hard work recovery takes. Recovery is difficult, takes a lot of time and requires commitment. It can be emotionally painful, lonely and exhausting. However, given the right circumstances, all systems can recover, whether they decide to choose 'final' fusion or functional multiplicity. Systems should be incredibly proud of their commitment and work towards healing and recovery.

In terms of how long systems are usually in therapy for, this varies for each system. Generally systems will be in longer-term therapy. This could be for a couple of years to ten years or sometimes more. Systems may be desperate to recover as quickly as possible. However, recovery cannot be rushed and it is important that systems take it at the right pace for them.

Medication

The treatment for DID and OSDD that is effective is long-term psychotherapy. Medication will not reverse the effects of having a separate personality. Medication cannot 'cure' DID or OSDD. It cannot get rid of alters. There is no medication proven to help with dissociation. However, there are medications that can be helpful for comorbid diagnoses or symptoms, such as antidepressants, anti-anxiety medication, antipsychotics and medications to help with sleep, nightmares or pain. Some systems take psychiatric medication but some do not. Psychiatric medication works for some systems and not for others. While it will not heal systems, it may help to reduce their comorbid symptoms.

Some systems find that different alters react differently to a medication, such as blocking the effects.[3] Some systems may be put on a variety of psychiatric medication to help them with their symptoms. Other systems find that they did not need to be on a medication or that they did not need to be on it long term. Pharmaceutical companies are profit-driven organisations and often promote their medications to GPs, primary healthcare providers and psychiatrists. This can influence the treatments that are recommended.

If there is a need for psychiatric medication and it helps, that is good. However, it is not essential for all systems.

OUR EXPERIENCE

We thought mental health medication was like physical health medication – if your doctor told you it would help, you took it. However, we have learned that it is a lot more nuanced with psychiatric medication. We wish we had not taken it for years. It helped in the beginning, but what we needed was our DID diagnosis so we could get specialist therapy. Taking anti-anxiety medication was sometimes helpful for us; however, we personally found that taking psychiatric medication got in the way of our therapy work and internal communication. We decided to prioritise our therapy work and have since found that having therapy for our DID has meant we have no need for medication. If we feel anxious, instead we will try and find out who feels this way and why. We realise medication can be very helpful for some systems, but for others it may not be needed.

CHAPTER 23

The Mental Health System

Mental Health Professionals

Some people with DID and OSDD may experience symptoms from their mental health that cause them to end up in hospitals, such as with self-harm or attempts on their life. It is up to each system to decide whether to disclose their DID/OSDD diagnosis to healthcare and/or mental health professionals. In an ideal world, disclosing multiplicity to healthcare professionals would result in a better chance of being understood; however, sadly this is not always the case.

Unfortunately mental health professionals are also affected by the stigma. Be mindful that they may not believe that DID or OSDD exist or may not believe that you have it. Some mental health professionals have never even heard of DID or OSDD. Being told you do not have DID/OSDD, or that it does not exist, can be damaging and systems deserve so much better. There is clearly a gap in the training of mental health professionals when it comes to dissociation, dissociative disorders, DID and OSDD.

Some professionals may be understanding of your diagnosis; however, some might not be. There is a mental health crisis nationwide and those with DID or OSDD may face even more difficulty in accessing understanding and treatment. Unfortunately some mental health professionals may be unprofessional in their job. Remember that you do not have to disclose anything about your life if you do not feel comfortable doing so. You do not have to tell anyone what your trauma is, even if they ask. (The only time it may be helpful would be during an assessment for dissociative disorders.) If you do reveal your trauma in an assessment, it may be safer to give a very brief synopsis, because going into any more detail could be triggering. A good mental health professional will not ask you to talk about your trauma in detail.

If you feel that a mental health professional has acted or spoken in an inappropriate way, tell someone you trust. If you wish, you could also make a complaint. Systems deserve professionalism when it comes to their care.

However, there *are* mental health professionals who care about systems, and who dedicate their lives to helping them. There are mental health professionals who are trauma-informed, trained in dissociative disorders, knowledgeable about multiplicity and experienced in working with people who have DID or OSDD. There are many mental health professionals out there who can help systems recover.

Psychiatric Hospitals

Some people with DID and OSDD have had or may experience psychiatric hospital inpatient admissions. Unfortunately there can be issues with psychiatric hospitals worldwide, including in the UK and US. Sometimes they can be unhelpful and sometimes they can make people worse. Psychiatric hospitals may be traumatic places to stay due to the other unwell patients and a lack of care from some staff. In the UK they are more suited for conditions that can be treated with medication, such as schizophrenia and bipolar.

However, psychiatric inpatient admissions can be helpful as a last resort if you are very unwell and cannot look after yourselves, are a risk to yourselves and your life or are a risk to others. You do not need to feel ashamed or embarrassed about staying in a psychiatric hospital and it does not make you a bad person. At the same time, being admitted to a psychiatric ward does not make your illness more valid than someone who has not been an inpatient. Psychiatric wards may sometimes be romanticised on social media; however, this is not the reality. Psychiatric inpatient stays may be hard for systems.

In the UK, there are two ways of being admitted to a psychiatric hospital. You can be a voluntary patient, where you agree to be hospitalised, or you can be detained/sectioned, where you are hospitalised even if you do not agree to it. This can change during your stay depending on the psychiatrist's assessment. If you are detained under the Mental Health Act 1983 you can be sectioned for up to 28 days (Section 2) and up to six months (Section 3).[1] You have a right to disagree with your section and the right to appeal it at a tribunal. Supposedly, as a voluntary patient you can leave whenever you want; however, this still is situational, and it is unlikely you can leave at night, or if the staff think it is too soon for you to leave.

Due to the lack of education among mental health professionals, ward staff may not understand the implications of your DID/OSDD. Some professionals may also not know what DID or OSDD are. This may make your system feel sad and invalidated. It is unfortunately not uncommon.

OUR EXPERIENCE

We have been an inpatient before. In our experience psychiatric hospitals are not the same as general hospitals, they do not always provide the same level of care and they do not always have a good understanding of what DID is. Hopefully one day this will change. Psychiatric hospitals should be places where systems can recover from a crisis and get the support they need.

What to Pack for Psychiatric Hospital

Psychiatric hospital admissions can happen unexpectedly, so you may not have time to pack before being admitted. Hospitals usually provide the basics needed for a stay, such as hospital pyjamas, shower products, a towel and a toothbrush. If you can, ask someone you know to bring in some belongings for you such as:

- **Clothes** – underwear, pyjamas, comfy clothes, cosy jumper, some shoes without laces.

- **Toiletries** – toothbrush, toothpaste, face wash, moisturiser, shower and sanitary products, hairbrush and bands, flip-flops to wear in the shower, makeup such as mascara, deodorant.

- **Comfort and distraction** – soft toy/stuffy for littles, your favourite book, a magazine, grounding tools, puzzle books such as a word search, crosswords or sudoku, colouring books and pens or pencils, a notebook/your journal, some nice snacks, earplugs to block out noise, origami and – if allowed – paints, knitting, games console, headphones.

- **Miscellaneous** – some money, re-useable coffee cup, water bottle.

Tips for Systems Who Are an Inpatient

Psychiatric wards are different all over the world and different within the same hospital. They each have different rules. For example, some psychiatric wards in the US do not allow phones, whereas in the UK they usually do. Here are some tips that may help your stay feel a little easier:

When You First Arrive

- Find out what time meals are. In the UK the typical mealtimes may be 08:00 Breakfast, 12:00 Lunch, 17:00 Dinner, 21:00 Supper, or something similar to this.

- If you take regular medication, let the staff know as soon as you arrive as they may need to order it and this could take some time. The hospitals usually dispense medication in the morning, after lunch, after dinner and before bed.

+ If you have any dietary requirements, e.g. are coeliac or a vegan, let the staff know. They should be able to cater for this; however, it may take a while to go through, so the sooner the better.

General Tips

+ Know your rights if you have been sectioned/detained. There are advocacy charities that can help provide legal information, advice and support, like attending ward round meetings with you (meetings with the hospital staff and sometimes psychiatrists).

+ Wards can be noisy. If you cannot get to sleep, you may want to ask the staff for medication to help. Sleep is important when you are unwell.

+ Having visitors can be something to look forward to. Find out the visiting times from the staff.

+ If doctors want to put you on a new medication, read and research the side effects.

+ Find out if you can be referred to a service that provides therapy; tell the staff in ward rounds that you feel this could really help with your recovery.

+ You may not be allowed phone chargers; however, you may be allowed a charger with a very short cable. The staff may also be able to charge your phone in their office; doing this overnight means you can use it during the day.

- It may feel difficult but try to wash daily, brush your hair and put on clean clothes, as it can make such a difference.

- Some systems may have poor memory. Write down notes from the ward rounds.

- It may be hard to fill time on the ward. Most wards will have some form of activities or offer therapy such as group art therapy. Ask if you are unsure. Engaging in these activities can be a good distraction and may help you feel a little better.

The Hospital Environment

- If you are allowed, try to go outside once a day, even to the garden if they have one. This should help to clear your mind.

- You may hear alarms go off on the ward. This is usually a panic alarm; buttons for these may be situated throughout the hospital.

- If are staying in hospital for a while, putting up photos or pages from magazines in your room may help make it feel less clinical and more comforting.

Other Patients

- If you are on a mixed gender ward and it is triggering or you feel unsafe, ask if you can be moved to a female only/ male only ward.

- Connecting with others during your stay can help pass the time and provide mutual support. However, it's ok to set boundaries and take care when building relationships.

Staff

♦ Find a staff member you get on with and try to express how you are feeling to them before acting on intrusive thoughts or impulses.

♦ Staff may do 'checks' on you. Your bedroom door may have a window that they look through throughout the day, to check you are ok. They may also do this at night too. You also may or may not be able to lock your bedroom door.

♦ You may come across some friendly and some not so friendly staff on psychiatric wards.

♦ Ask if staff know how long your admission may be or if you have any leave (are allowed to leave the hospital for a bit, then return).

♦ Find out from other staff or patients if there are any other services in your local area that you could be referred to. If you do not have a care coordinator or are not part of a mental health team, you could ask about this.

CHAPTER 24

Crisis Management

Feeling Suicidal

Sadly, it is not uncommon for systems or alters to feel suicidal. Loewenstein states: 'In clinical studies, 92% to 100% of DID patients endorsed current or past suicidal ideation; 60% to 80% reported a history of suicide attempts.'[1] These are important statistics which should be taken very seriously.

Having suicidal alters can be scary for people with DID and OSDD; it is unlikely that everyone else in the system also wants their life to end. It can be scary coming-to after an attempt and not knowing why or how it happened. Although suicidal alters pose a high risk and it seems their intent is harmful, they may be trying to help. Even suicidal alters/systems may not want to die. Suicidal alters may be protectors who think that they are helping the system escape a difficult or painful situation. However, they may not be aware of the permanency of suicide. You can thank them for trying to help protect your system but inform them that these thoughts and behaviours are not helpful or protective. You can ask them not to act on these thoughts, to help protect your system.

Suicidal alters need to learn about healthy and alternative ways to protect the system. They must remember to be considerate of everyone in the system, such as remembering that the littles want and deserve to live. It may be difficult for other alters to intervene when a suicidal alter has made plans, but showing compassion, asking them to consider others, helping and exploring why they feel this way in therapy and having a thorough safety plan can all help.

If you notice that someone in your system has made life-ending plans, it is very important that you tell someone such as a therapist or suicide helpline. You may feel ashamed for feeling suicidal or scared to tell someone, but try to overlook this: your life is important. Things can get better. This intensity of emotion will pass. There are happy moments in your future waiting for you.

Suicidal alters may be one of the reasons why systems can be misdiagnosed with borderline personality disorder (BPD). Health professionals may see a history of suicide attempts and wrongly assume that this is BPD.

How to Get External Help If You Feel Suicidal

There are many ways that people with DID and OSDD can ask for help. If you can, it is helpful to tell those close to you who you trust, whether this is friends or family. It can also be helpful to tell your therapist, counsellor, teacher, school nurse, GP, primary healthcare provider, care coordinator, suicide or mental health helpline. If your life is at risk right now it is very important that you get help immediately. Call your country's emergency service number (999 in the UK and 911 in the US) or go straight to your nearest A&E/ER/hospital. If you can keep yourselves safe for a short time but you still need help, in England and Wales you can call NHS 111 and select option 2 for a 24/7 urgent mental health support helpline. Alternatively, contact your GP surgery/primary healthcare provider and request an emergency appointment[2] or go to an urgent treatment centre/urgent care centre. Additionally, there are crisis helplines that have text, phone and email options which can be found in the back of this book in the Recommended Resources.

You could say:

+ 'I'm/we're feeling suicidal.'
+ 'There is an alter in my system who is suicidal and I am scared that they might do something.'
+ 'One of the alters in my system has made plans to end our life.'
+ 'I'm really not feeling good. I do not feel safe.'

Write it down on a piece of paper or send it as a written phone message if you feel too scared to say the words out loud.

How to Cope with Suicidal Thoughts in a Mental Health Crisis
Identify Who Feels This Way

+ Identify who feels suicidal/is having a crisis.
+ Ask them why they feel this way. Was someone triggered? Are they or another alter stuck in a trauma memory?
+ Validate their feelings.
+ Acknowledge that they are likely trying to help, just in the wrong ways. Thank them for trying to protect the system but inform them that there are alternative ways to help.

Keeping Safe

+ Try to unblend with the alter who feels suicidal/is having a crisis.
+ If the alter fronting is the one feeling suicidal or experiencing a crisis, see if you can get another alter to switch with them, such as a protector. You may need to use a positive trigger. Suggest that the alter in crisis go to an internal safe or calm space in the inner world.
+ Go to a safe place in the real world.
+ Make sure your home is safe by removing or throwing away anything that could be harmful, such as asking someone else to look after your medication or giving your old medication to a pharmacy.

Distraction and Comfort

+ Distract yourselves by doing something that makes you happy, such as watching your favourite film, ordering your favourite takeaway, colouring-in, playing your favourite game or baking some cookies.

+ Comfort and self-soothe yourselves such as by putting on soft pyjamas, cuddling toys/stuffed animals or listening to happy or calm music.
+ Journal to help you understand your thoughts and feelings.
+ Remember that you have survived all your hardest days before. You are strong. You will get through this.

In an Emergency

+ If in immediate danger or your life is at risk, go to your nearest hospital/A&E/ER or call your country's emergency helpline.
+ Some systems may take prescribed medication to help them in a crisis.

People and Contacts

+ Tell someone how you feel. Tell them if you cannot keep yourselves safe.
+ Speak to a loved one on the phone, call a crisis helpline or contact your therapist. (See Recommended Resources for helpline numbers.)
+ Be with or around other people.

Remember

+ Remind your system internally and/or externally that we are safe now.
+ Try to delay acting on your thoughts, for an hour, for a day, for a week.
+ Remind the alter in crisis that other alters want to live.
+ Remember that no alter is bad or broken, even if they are

in pain. They are part of the same system and deserve help, not punishment.

Preparation (to be done before a crisis happens)

- *Create a safety plan.*
- *Give a copy of your safety plan to those close to you.*
- Some systems find having an emergency card they carry around with them is helpful. These cards include information on DID/OSDD and their emergency contact. If in crisis, this card can be shown to someone. The author of this book has created DID and OSDD emergency cards (see the Recommended Resources).
- Write a list of alters who have felt suicidal or experienced a crisis before. Write a list of alters who could help and front during a crisis.
- Some systems find a list of signs that you are becoming more unwell/approaching a crisis can be helpful.
- Some people put helpline phone numbers into the contacts on their phone, so that they are easily accessible in difficult moments.
- Create a hospital support plan if it's something you may need. This could include some information on DID/OSDD. The author of this book has created a short leaflet guide to DID and OSDD which could be used. (For more information see the Recommended Resources.)

Crisis Toolbox

Some people with DID and OSDD find a crisis toolbox helpful during difficult times. To create one, find a medium-sized box, such as a shoe box, wooden box or plastic box. Fill it with things that can comfort alters in your system. Here are some examples of things to include:

Essentials

- Crisis/suicide helplines
- Safety/crisis plan
- Phone numbers of loved ones
- First aid kit (if your system self-harms)

Grounding Items

- A list of different grounding techniques
- Fidget toys
- Nice smells such as perfume or essential oils
- Grounding stones
- A candle

Comforting Items

- Soft toys/stuffed animal for littles
- Picture books for littles
- Photos of loved ones/letters/postcards
- Fluffy socks
- Favourite chocolate/sweet/snack/tea
- A face mask
- A bath bomb
- A letter to yourselves

Distracting Items

- Colouring books and pens/pencils
- A book of yoga poses/affirmations/poetry
- A small watercolour paint set
- A pack of cards
- Your favourite magazine(s)

Template of a Safety/Crisis Plan

A crisis plan is a helpful resource to reach to in times of need. A crisis plan can be helpful for when a system feels suicidal, wants to harm themselves or has experienced flashbacks, body memories or remembered trauma.

Our Safety Plan

What to do if in immediate danger or if we cannot keep ourselves safe: (e.g. where is the nearest hospital?)

People we can call:

Helplines we can contact:

Ways to distract ourselves:

Ways to comfort ourselves:

Helpful quotes/affirmations/words of advice/reasons to live:

How to keep ourselves safe:

Alters who can help or switch:

What has helped us in the past when we felt this way?

What would we tell another system who is feeling this way?

Notes:

Mental Health Crisis

At times, people with DID and OSDD may experience a mental health crisis. Sometimes when a system feels distressed or in crisis it is due to an alter being triggered. For example, a little was triggered and felt overwhelmed which resulted in a suicidal alter fronting to try and 'help'. Sometimes it may be possible to self-soothe and prevent an alter acting in a harmful way. Other times more measures may be needed to help keep the system safe.

Knowing what to do in a mental health crisis is very important. Having a crisis plan can be extremely helpful. Some people also like to give their crisis plan to those close to them such as friends or family, so they know how to respond in an emergency. Some people also have a crisis toolbox. It is ok to experience a mental health crisis, you will get through it. Over time, through help in therapy, systems can stop experiencing mental health crises or can experience them less frequently. Systems can learn how to manage difficult situations before they become a crisis and their coping skills can become second nature.

Mental health crises can be difficult to experience but help is always available and in a variety of different forms. It can be helpful to create a safety plan when you are not in a crisis, ensuring you are prepared for the possibility of one happening out of the blue. Over time, you will learn which coping mechanisms work best for your system. Finally, remember that the crisis will not last forever, your life matters and your life is important.

CHAPTER 25

Self-Help

Grounding Techniques

Dissociation causes people to float away from reality. Grounding is the opposite of dissociation. Grounding techniques can help you to ground yourselves and come back into the present. These techniques are especially helpful for managing dissociation, depersonalisation and derealisation, but they can also help with anxiety, panic attacks, flashbacks and intense emotions. Here are some different ideas for you to try. Systems may find that some grounding techniques work for them, while others do not, so it can be helpful to try out different methods. You can highlight the techniques which work best for you in the lists below. It can also be helpful to carry a list of grounding techniques or cards with you in your bag.

5-4-3-2-1

The classic 5-4-3-2-1 exercise. Name:

> **5** Five things you can see.
> **4** Four things you can feel.
> **3** Three things you can hear.
> **2** Two things you can smell.
> **1** One thing you can taste.

Sight

- ✦ Do some colouring-in, doodling, drawing or painting.

- Do a jigsaw puzzle, crossword, word search or sudoku.
- Do some photography, origami or flower arranging.
- Play cards, a board game, a video game or play with toys.
- Look at the sky, clouds and trees.
- List everything in your surroundings like the chair, table, book...
- Decide on a shape like a square or circle. Look for as many examples of this shape in your surroundings that you can.
- Choose a colour like red or yellow. Look for as many examples of this colour in your surroundings that you can.

Sound

- Talk out loud to yourselves, sing, whistle or hum.
- Listen to calm music.
- Speak to someone in person or on the phone.
- Play a musical instrument.
- Listen to your breathing.
- Listen to the sounds around you, like birds, chatting or cars.
- Do a guided mindfulness or meditation exercise.

Taste

- Drink some water.
- Have a warm drink like a tea, coffee or hot chocolate.
- Have a cold drink like a juice, smoothie or iced matcha.
- Eat something crunchy, like cereal.
- Eat something minty, like a mint, or chew on some gum.
- Eat something spicy, like chilli noodles.
- Eat something sour, like a sour candy.
- Eat something strong, like an orange or dark chocolate.

Touch

- Stretch, do some yoga, wiggle your fingers and toes or shake your limbs.

- Put your hands under running water or hold an ice cube.
- Walk on grass or sand with bare feet or press your feet firmly on the ground.
- Touch different textures around you and describe them.
- Hug yourselves, try the butterfly hug, hug a loved one or hold their hand.
- Stroke a cat, dog or other pet or hug a soft toy (stuffed animal).
- Hold a grounding stone. Pick a stone that feels nice to hold and carry it around with you.
- Play with a sensory toy like a Tangle.[1]
- Put on a soft jumper or wrap yourselves in a soft blanket.
- Jog on the spot or do star jumps (jumping jacks).
- Sew, knit, collage, write, journal or sculpt clay.
- Clap your hands or play catch.
- Do some model making, jewellery making or wood working.
- Clean, re-organise or wash up.
- Do some gardening, woodworking or a DIY project.
- Kick a football, shoot some hoops or go skateboarding.
- Braid or style your hair or paint your nails.
- Dance, go rock climbing or go cycling.
- Some systems like to do tapping such as Emotional Freedom Techniques (EFT) tapping.

Smell

- Smell something strong, like coffee or essential oils.
- Smell some fresh herbs, like basil or lavender, or smell a flower.
- Smell some fresh air outside.
- Do some baking or cooking.
- Light a scented candle.
- Spray some perfume, deodorant, colognes or aftershave.

Other

+ Tell yourselves, we are safe now.
+ Remind yourselves that you are in the present. Look at and say the date, where you are and what you are doing (e.g. 'It's Tuesday 4th June 2026. We are in our kitchen, we are safe and we are stroking our fluffy cat').
+ Have a system check-in. Ask inside if anyone needs anything or if there is anything you can do to help.

Grounding may feel unhelpful or overwhelming for some systems, especially in the beginning of their healing journey. Instead, when systems are triggered, they may prefer to ask inside who is triggered, why and how the system can help, and focus on ensuring internal and external safety and comfort. For some, a combination of grounding and internal communication works best.

TIPS FOR SUPPORTING PEOPLE WITH DID AND OSDD
Help systems to ground themselves if they are dissociating, having a flashback or having a panic attack. This could be by offering them some water, telling them they are safe now, reminding them what year it is, prompting the 5-4-3-2-1 skill, asking if they would like a hug or doing an activity with them such as baking or going on a walk.

Helpful Skills

There are some skills from certain types of therapy that can also be helpful for systems, such as skills from cognitive behavioural therapy (CBT) or dialectical behaviour therapy (DBT). The recommended therapy for DID and OSDD is specialised talking therapy, but CBT and DBT skills may be helpful additions. An example of a helpful skill is opposite action. If you want an emotion to go away or become less intense, do the opposite action of it. For example, if you are feeling depressed and are isolating yourselves, do the opposite action, like socialising or going outside and interacting with others. It can feel like a difficult thing to do, but it can really help you to feel better. For details on CBT and DBT resources, see the Recommended Resources.

System Affirmations

Affirmations are encouraging statements people repeat to themselves to promote a more positive way of thinking and gently reframe negative thoughts. Over time, through the brain's neuroplasticity, affirmations can support changes in thought patterns, helping to build self-esteem, resilience and emotional wellbeing.

- ◆ I am important and my system cares about me so much.
- ◆ I am never alone; my system is always here for me.
- ◆ We are allowed to feel all of our feelings. They are real and they matter.
- ◆ We are safe now. Our system will always protect us.
- ◆ It's ok to need help and comfort. Our needs are never too much.
- ◆ Our pain is real and valid.
- ◆ We have survived all of our hardest days so far, that's a good track record.
- ◆ All of us are worthy of love, kindness and understanding.
- ◆ We are clever, creative and kind. Our imagination is beautiful.
- ◆ We are proud of our system and the progress we've made.
- ◆ We are so loved, just as we are.
- ◆ Our trauma was not our fault and it does not define us. We are more than what happened to us.
- ◆ We are grateful for our alters. Our multiplicity is a superpower.
- ◆ We have agency now. We can set boundaries and say no.

- ◆ We are learning to listen and work as a team. Together we can create system harmony.
- ◆ We are not broken. Our alters were created to protect us and our dissociation helped us to survive.
- ◆ We are allowed to play, have fun and be silly!
- ◆ We belong to a worldwide community of systems who care and understand.
- ◆ Healing is not linear and that's ok. We are allowed to take things at our own pace and in our own time.
- ◆ Together, we are healing and growing. Together, we can recover.
- ◆ Our future is bright and good things are waiting for us!

Complementary Ways to Heal from Trauma

If accessible, specialised talking therapy should be the main form of treatment for people with DID and OSDD. However, sometimes additional methods can be helpful too. Different methods work for different people and have varying levels of success and preference. For people who are unable to access specialised talking therapy for DID/OSDD, they may also find these methods helpful.

Some complementary healing methods include:

- ◆ (trauma-informed) yoga
- ◆ support groups
- ◆ mindfulness and meditation
- ◆ breathwork
- ◆ massage
- ◆ Tai Chi
- ◆ tapping (Emotional Freedom Technique)
- ◆ acupuncture
- ◆ sleep hygiene
- ◆ spending time in nature
- ◆ dance
- ◆ journalling

+ gratitude journalling.

Yoga

Yoga can help with trauma recovery. It supports feeling present, connected and safe in your body, and can help ease dissociation. It is gentle and mindful. Implementing yoga into your daily or weekly routine can be beneficial. Systems may feel scared or reluctant to do yoga; this is ok. It may be difficult for systems to feel present in their body while doing yoga, due to trauma that is stored in the body or depersonalisation making them feel disconnected to their body. If this is the case, take things slowly. Try doing just one yoga pose that feels safe to you, then slowly introduce more. You could try some short yoga sessions; there are lots of great yoga videos on You-Tube. Or you could go to an in-person yoga class. Trauma-informed yoga may be more helpful for people with DID and OSDD and it is available both online and in person. Focusing on your breath while doing yoga poses can feel healing and calming. When practising yoga it can be helpful to remember that you have agency and you can stop at any time.

Mindfulness

Mindfulness is about being present and aware of the current moment. Mindfulness can help with everyone's mental health. It is particularly helpful for people with mental health conditions. People with DID and OSDD can experience severe dissociation and mindfulness can help counteract this by keeping you grounded. Incorporating mindfulness into your life can help with recovery. Sometimes mindfulness may seem unfamiliar or scary, and that's completely ok. It is not the same as meditation. Mindfulness is also not a spiritual or religious practice. It may feel difficult for systems because being in the present may feel overwhelming. It is something that you can practise slowly and in your own time.

How to Be Mindful

Being mindful means being curious and noticing your surroundings. There are many mindfulness exercises you can try, but you can also bring mindfulness to everyday activities like going on a walk, doing the washing up, riding a bike, going on a train journey or talking to a friend. It is about fully engaging in the present and not being distracted by thoughts about the past or future.

You can do mindfulness exercises that focus on one or all of your senses. Here is an example:

Using your five senses, mindfully drink your tea and describe your experience

What does it look like?	What does it taste like?	Can you hear yourself sip the tea?	Can you smell the tea?	Can you feel the mug in your hand?
What colour is it? What colour is the mug?	Sweet? Bitter?	Focus on the sounds.	What does it smell of?	Where? Is it hot? Smooth?

It is ok if you get distracted from the task or start dissociating, just bring your focus back. You may start thinking about the past or the future, like thinking *What should I have for dinner?* Just push these thoughts aside or let them float away.

Mindfulness Exercises

+ Mindfully listen to all the sounds that you can hear. Name them. Can you hear birds? Talking? Your breath? Cars? The wind? Music? Your heartbeat...?

+ Try something new or different like brushing your teeth with your non-dominant hand, walking a different route, making a new recipe or writing a poem. Notice what feels different.

+ Mindfully engage with a grape, another piece of food or

a drink, like a cup of tea. Notice and describe how it feels, smells, tastes, sounds and looks.

+ Sit comfortably; close your eyes if you wish. Notice your thoughts arise, picture them floating down a river or passing by on a motorway. Don't cling onto the thought, just let it go.

+ Do some mindful colouring, painting, drawing, mending, cleaning, woodworking or any other activity that uses your hands. Don't give yourself any other distraction. Fully engage in the activity.

Gratitude Lists and Glimmers

Gratitude lists can be helpful for people with DID and OSDD. Some systems like to write them daily and others may find them helpful to do when they are feeling low. Some people also like to keep a gratitude journal. You could write a list of things that you are grateful for, good things that happened to you today, things that made you happy, things you are proud of doing or interesting things you noticed today. These examples do not have to be grand. It can feel good to notice and appreciate the small, magical moments that bring you joy. These moments can often be overlooked. Some people refer to these moments as glimmers. Glimmers are the opposite of triggers. You could also keep a glimmer journal.

You may want to think of three, five or ten examples at a time.

Some Examples

Today we are grateful for/Today's glimmers:

+ The warm sun
+ Cups of tea
+ Our body that can take us places
+ Seeing cute dogs

◆ Having a shelter over our head.

Things to Be Proud of

For some people with DID and OSDD, getting through each day can be difficult. You should be proud of getting through each day and completing your daily tasks. You should be proud of getting out of bed, going to therapy and cooking dinner. Productivity does not define your value or dictate your worth. You deserve to feel proud of navigating life as a system, which is no easy feat. People who have not experienced childhood trauma often have a head start in life.

Self-Care

Self-care does not have to be all about face masks and bubble baths. Though these can be nice sometimes, doing even the basic daily tasks can be difficult when you have DID or OSDD. You should be proud of yourselves for achieving even one or two daily self-care tasks. Over time you can build these up. It is important to try and do 'simple' self-care daily. Indulgent self-care can be done when you feel you need it, such as when you are going through a crisis or are having a hard day. Everyone will have different self-care preferences but here are some ideas to consider:

'Simple' Daily Self-Care

◆ Making your bed
◆ Washing your face
◆ Brushing your teeth
◆ Getting changed out of your pyjamas
◆ Having a shower
◆ Brushing your hair
◆ Drinking water
◆ Eating three meals
◆ Doing the washing up

- ✦ Getting some fresh air
- ✦ Writing in your journal
- ✦ Doing something you enjoy
- ✦ Taking your medication
- ✦ Getting a good night's sleep

Indulgent Self-Care

- ✦ Having a long shower or bubble bath
- ✦ Going to the cinema, art gallery or museum
- ✦ Buying yourselves flowers or a new house plant
- ✦ Organising your kitchen or decluttering your closet
- ✦ Making your favourite hot drink (like hot chocolate)
- ✦ Doing yoga, going on a bike ride or run
- ✦ Making or buying your favourite meal or dessert
- ✦ Doing a face mask or getting a massage

PART 6

Supporting Systems

CHAPTER 26

Advice for Friends, Family and Partners

Tips for Friends, Family and Partners
(How to Support People with DID and OSDD)

+ **Take things easy.** Learning that someone you love has DID or OSDD can be unexpected. It's completely normal to feel angry or sad knowing that they experienced childhood trauma and to feel confused about their condition. Try to take things slowly, be patient and learn about things at your own pace. With time you can process this information and develop a better understanding.

+ **Education.** Try to learn as much as you can about DID/OSDD through reliable sources. The more you learn, the easier it will be to understand. Having someone who understands your mental health condition is extremely valuable. You could start by reading books about trauma, dissociation and DID/OSDD, preferably those which were written recently. You could also watch educational videos and documentaries, listen to educational podcasts and research charities or organisations dedicated to this subject. See the Recommended Resources at the end of this book for more information.

+ **Be empathetic and understanding.** Recognise that it must be challenging at times to live with DID/OSDD. Remember that having multiple alters allowed this person to survive.

+ **Listen.** Let them know that you are open to learning anything about their DID/OSDD, if they would like to share. If they do, be a good listener.

+ **Get to know the system and each alter individually.** If the system feels comfortable and trusts you, they may let you get to know their system and meet other alters. This is a privilege. If a system does not feel comfortable speaking about other alters or the other alters do not introduce themselves, this is fine too and does not mean they do not trust you. It is up to each system when/if they ever feel ready to tell you more. It can be daunting to share and some systems find it easier not to.

+ **Treat everyone equally.** Treat all the alters in the system with equal respect and kindness.

+ **Be conscious of littles.** Littles are child alters who usually act and think like a child. If they front, speak to them like you would speak to a real child: kindly and in an age appropriate way. It may be scary and confusing for a little when they front. They are a child in an adult's body; this may feel strange. Reassure them and help keep them safe. It can help to stay with them if you are out in public, as they may need your support and not know how to get home on their own. If it is not appropriate or safe for them to be fronting, ask them politely if they could switch with an adult alter.

+ **If you think someone has switched, you can ask them** if you would like to. Respect them if they do not feel comfortable saying.

+ **Be kind.** Having DID and OSDD can be difficult. Systems may have to take life at a slower pace and that is ok. It could mean that they are unable to work for a while or it could mean that they may go to a psychiatric hospital to help keep them safe for a while. No one deserves to be hurt as a child and the consequences can be complex to live with. Be patient with the system you know. Be aware that they may be in therapy for a while and that recovery can be long and hard. Systems can recover though, and live fulfilled lives. Having a loving support network can make all the difference.

+ **Be prepared for emotional fluctuations** and shifts in a system's behaviour. Some systems may find it harder to regulate their emotions, especially when they have child alters. Different alters may also interact differently with other people, such as some who are shyer.

+ **Show interest.** Show that you are interested in their life such as by asking questions. It is nice when someone shows interest. Be respectful if they do not want to answer your question. *Never* expect or force a system to disclose their trauma to you.

+ **Be aware and avoid a system's triggers,** if they feel comfortable letting you know. It is ok if they do not.

+ **Show them love and support.** Show them you care about them, such as by checking in with them regularly by sending them a text message.

+ **Don't force it.** Never try and force a particular alter to front (be in control of the body) even if you want to or want to speak to a particular alter. Do not use positive or negative triggers to do this. It is not up to you who fronts in their system. Do not force anything the system is not comfortable with.

- **Remember that many of the behaviours or responses that systems have are a result of their trauma.** They may not be able to control this, they may not want to respond in these ways; they are not purposefully being difficult. This also means some of their reactions come from child alters, who may not have learned how to deal with difficult situations yet. Even if there is not a child alter fronting, the system may respond like a child, such as being more sensitive. Try to keep this in mind, be patient and not take things personally.

- **Help them get help.** Suggest therapy or mental health support if they do not already have this. You could ask if they would like your help to find a therapist.

- **Advocate for them.** Support and help systems, such as by advocating for them in medical situations if they would like your support.

- **Respect a system's privacy** such as by respecting them if they do not want to speak about their system or being a system. Do not repeat something a system has shared with you to others.

- **Ask if they would like any practical help** such as help organising their weekly meals or picking them up from their therapy session.

- **Try not to judge.** The fictional media representations of DID/OSDD can be inaccurate and misinformed. Do not use them as your reference. DID and OSDD are *not* like the movie *Split*. Systems are more likely to be the victim of a crime than the perpetrator. Having DID or OSDD does not make someone a bad person. Systems do not choose to have these conditions. They have them due to childhood trauma. It is not their fault, so do not blame or judge them.

◆ **Think about the language you use.** Using words such as 'crazy', 'insane', 'maniac' or 'psycho' in your day-to-day conversations can upset some systems. Mental health conditions are not something to villainise, mock or make fun of. These words only perpetuate the stigma. Never use these words to describe someone with DID or OSDD.

◆ **Be aware of them going into a crisis or feeling suicidal** and know how to help. It can be helpful to have a copy of their crisis plan or know what to do if a crisis happens. It can also be useful to know how to help them with other difficult experiences, such as panic attacks or flashbacks. To learn about these, you can read chapters 11 and 12.

◆ **Ask how you can help them.** If you are unsure about how to help, just ask. Such as by asking how you can best support them/about boundaries/if they need help or need to leave somewhere. It is also ok if the system does not feel like sharing.

◆ **Stand up for them** and for other systems, such as by calling others out if they speak about systems in a negative way or spread incorrect information.

◆ **Educate others about DID and OSDD.** If you feel comfortable, speak to others you know about DID/OSDD or share the resources you have found useful, such as on social media.

How to Speak Kindly and Respectfully to a System

Not everyone knows what to say when speaking with a system. Some examples of how you might show support and are listed below.

◆ 'Thank you for trusting me with the information that you are a system, I really appreciate it.'

- 'I look forward to meeting other alters in your system if this happens.'
- 'Do you mind if I ask about your system? It's fine if not.'
- 'If you feel comfortable sharing, I was wondering who I have met in your system?'
- 'If you don't mind saying, may I ask who is fronting now?'
- 'Are there any ways I can support you if someone else fronts?'
- 'Would you like me to use different names or pronouns with different alters?'
- 'If the littles would ever like to play a game, I would love to play with them.'
- 'I am so sorry to hear you experienced childhood trauma. I am here if you ever need anything.'
- 'Is there anything you think could be helpful for me to know about your system or mental health?'
- 'Is there anything grounding or comforting I can offer you if you need it?'
- 'I care about all of you so much.'

How to Help a System During or After a Trigger/Flashback/Panic Attack/Body Memory/When a Trauma Memory Arises

Here are some ideas of things you could try. Different methods may work for different systems. You do not need to do all these things at once.

General Tips

- Be a calming presence, show them kindness and validate them. Try not to bombard them with too many questions.
- It is ok if they just want to be alone. It may help to occasionally check in on them.
- Educate yourself on what these experiences are (e.g. read the sections of this book which explain them).

+ When they are not experiencing these symptoms, you may want to make a plan with them on how you can best help them if this happens (again).

What to Say

+ Tell them that you are sorry that they are experiencing this.
+ Remind them that they are safe now and remind them of the current year.
+ Suggest they take a break from their work/regular routine, if needed and if possible.

What to Ask

+ Ask if they would like to go somewhere calm and quiet, such as sitting on the sofa.
+ Ask them if they would like a hug, to hold your hand or for you to stay with them.
+ Ask if they can keep themselves safe.
+ Ask if they would like to talk about it or not; if not, respect this.
+ Ask if there is anything that you could do to help.

How to Help

+ Offer some ways they could comfort themselves, such as would they like a cosy jumper, fluffy blanket or a soft toy/ stuffed animal.
+ Suggest some forms of distraction, such as would they like to watch television or a movie with you, go on a short walk with you, do some colouring in together or cook or bake together.
+ Help them to ground themselves by suggesting a grounding exercise, such as the 5-4-3-2-1 exercise. Help prompt them with this, like asking *Can you name 5 things you can see? Etc...*

+ Offer them practical help with things, such as by making them dinner or a warm drink.

How to Help a System Who Is Suicidal/Is Experiencing a Crisis

+ If they have made an attempt, are planning to or their life is at risk, go to your nearest hospital/A&E/ER or call 999/911/your country's emergency number/an ambulance immediately.
+ If you are not sure if a system is feeling suicidal, ask, or ask if they can keep themselves safe.
+ If you are worried about them, you could accompany them to your nearest hospital, call NHS 111, call your local urgent mental health helpline (which can be found online) or get an emergency GP/primary healthcare provider appointment.

What to Ask

+ Ask if they would like to talk about how they feel. Be understanding if they do not want to.
+ Ask if there is anything you could do right now to help or help them feel safe.
+ Ask if you can see their safety/crisis plan or have a copy of it. (If they do not have one, you could suggest they make one at a later date when they are more stable.)
+ Ask if they would find going to a crisis cafe or support hub helpful, or a crisis/recovery house (short-term accommodation for a mental health crisis).
+ Ask if they would like something to eat or a warm drink.
+ Suggest they call a helpline.

What to Do

- Make sure they are in a safe place.
- Ensure you remain calm and act quickly. Try not to get angry at them or blame them.
- Remove anything that they could use to hurt themselves such as their medication.
- Keep an eye on them. Ask if you could do something together like watch television or do some colouring-in.

What to Say

- 'It is very brave of you to reach out.'
- 'I will do my best to help you get through this.'
- 'You are not alone; I am here for you and I love and care about you.'
- 'I am so sorry you are feeling this way.'
- 'Validate their feelings.'
- 'Do *not* tell them to cheer up, think more positively, be grateful for what they have or tell them they are silly.'

How to Support Yourself

- Speak to your loved ones, friends and family.
- Consider joining a carer's support group for people who know someone with a mental illness.
- Find ways to de-stress, such as with yoga or journalling.
- Speak to a helpline.
- Consider letting your work know. Take time off work if you can/think it would help.
- Validate yourself. It is completely normal to be feeling overwhelmed/scared/worried or out of control.
- Be kind and patient with yourself, and give yourself grace.

- ◆ Consider getting professional help, such as seeing a counsellor or therapist.
- ◆ If you are feeling very depressed or anxious, consider psychiatric medication.

CHAPTER 27

Advice for Professionals

Many different professionals can encounter people with DID and OSDD, so it is important for them to be aware of these conditions. It is especially important for mental health professionals such as psychiatrists, psychotherapists, psychologists, occupational therapists, social workers, counsellors, mental health nurses and mental health support workers. Other professions in which knowledge on DID and OSDD could be helpful include GPs, doctors, nurses, teachers, lawyers, police officers and HR professionals. It can also be helpful for all organisations and businesses to know about DID and OSDD as they may have employees or clients who have these conditions.

Being Trauma-Informed

It is very important that professionals who work with vulnerable people are trauma-informed. You are not trauma-informed until you understand all mental health conditions related to trauma. This includes DID and OSDD. Both these mental health conditions are formed due to childhood trauma. Professionals cannot claim to be trauma-informed if they do not know about DID and OSDD.

Those who work with vulnerable people include teachers, healthcare professionals and those working with children, with the elderly, in the prison system and in mental health.

Being trauma-informed means understanding the risks and impact of trauma. It enables you to best support everyone by recognising the signs of trauma and knowing what to look out for.

This awareness helps you prevent, respond to and address trauma effectively, allowing you to contribute to keeping people safe.

Advice for Mental Health Professionals

- ◆ If your professional qualification does not teach you about DID or OSDD, or teaches you very little about these conditions, it can be helpful to do extra training and research. In their article on DID in *The British Journal of Psychiatry*, Reinders and Veltman state 'that information in undergraduate and graduate textbooks about trauma and dissociation is inadequate or simply wrong'.[1]

- ◆ For most people with DID and OSDD, their multiplicity is not obvious and you may not see evidence of it. This does not mean that they are faking it. DID and OSDD often develop covertly as a protective mechanism.

- ◆ It is important for mental health professionals to believe people who have DID and OSDD. Only a minuscule minority of people may pretend to have these conditions, the vast majority are telling the truth and need your support.

- ◆ Recognise that working with people with DID and OSDD will be different to working with people who have other mental health conditions.

- ◆ Do not ask a system for details of their trauma unless this is needed for a diagnostic assessment. Asking for details could cause them to get triggered and potentially have a mental health crisis.

- ◆ People with DID and OSDD may react differently to psychiatric medications compared to non-systems.

◆ Some systems are unable to access a DID/OSDD diagnosis for a range of reasons. If someone is not diagnosed, do not assume they are faking. Remember that all diagnosed DID and OSDD systems were once undiagnosed.

◆ Be patient, kind and understanding.

Advice for Therapists
Working with Systems

◆ If you do not know much about DID and OSDD, that is ok. You can learn about these conditions. Being aware of dissociative disorders and systems is important, it can help you spot these symptoms in clients you may have, allowing you to give them the best care or redirect them to someone else who can.

◆ It is highly recommended that you complete training on DID and OSDD if you would like to work with systems. Even if you are not treating a system, getting professional training on DID and OSDD is a good idea; a client you are working with may be a system but not yet know.

◆ Treating a system may seem strange at first. Try to put your judgements aside and welcome all alters.

◆ Be open to learning from systems who are your clients.

◆ Systems are not scary or dangerous; they just want your help to recover.

◆ It can be helpful to ask your client's system for a list of alters and/or their alter profiles. This allows you to keep track of everyone in their system and get to know everyone.

- Treat all alters equally and allow all alters time in therapy. Do not insist on speaking only to the host, if there is one. It is important that all alters are involved in therapy. Without everyone being involved, full recovery is not possible.

- Keep in mind that a system's amnesia means they may not remember what you spoke about in any of your previous sessions, whether it was the same alter who attended or a different one(s). Additionally, alters who have not yet met you may not recognise you. They may see you as a stranger, even if you have been working with the system for a long time.

- Be careful speaking about (details of) trauma with all the alters in the system. Some alters may not know anything about the system's trauma, even if other alters do. The same goes for not sharing intimate conversations you have had with other alters.

- Some therapists who work in person like to have a box on hand with children's toys, sensory toys or grounding tools.

Different Alters

- Ask for an alter's pronouns (e.g. she/her, he/him, they/them) and try your best to remember to use the right pronouns. Systems can have alters of different genders and it is not nice being misgendered.

- Be aware that you may meet a different alter in every session.

- Switches are not always obvious. If you think there may have been a switch, just ask. Such as by saying, 'It feels like there may have been a switch. Is that right?', 'Hello! May I ask who's here with me now?' or, if you are speaking to someone new, 'Hi there! It's lovely to meet you. I'm (your name), the therapist working with your system. What's your name?' Note that not all alters will know their name or have a name.

- If child alters (littles) front, introduce yourself, explain that you are their system's therapist and you're here to help them. Speak to child as you would to real children, using simple, warm language and be extra friendly and approachable to help make them feel comfortable. Reassure them that this is a safe space. Some child alters may find it easier to communicate through alternative forms, such as art or play.

- Different alters may have different attachment styles and can behave differently. Some might keep a bit of a distance, while others, like littles, may seek connection and reassurance. This is completely normal. Child alters often want to feel heard and supported. Other alters may be less trusting, fearful or hesitant about therapy, because of past trauma.

- Specific alters may deal with their own mental health conditions, such as an alter who has an eating disorder.

System Recovery

- A professional and trusting therapeutic relationship is a crucial foundation to allow for successful trauma work and system recovery.

- All systems are different and can take different amounts of time to recover.

- When working with DID and OSDD clients, it is up to each individual system to decide on their recovery destination. It is not for their therapist to decide. They may want 'final' fusion, they may want functional multiplicity, or they might not yet know which route they would like to take. All three options are valid and as a therapist you should respect a system's decision and support them regardless. A therapist should not force 'final' fusion on systems if they do not want this.

◆ Do not force or encourage a system to remember their trauma or share details if they are not ready. This should only happen when the system feels comfortable and chooses to talk about it.

◆ Encourage alter communication as this can help systems in their recovery journey.

◆ The frequency of therapy sessions can vary between different systems. For example, systems may have therapy biweekly, once a week or more than once a week. Different intervals work best for different systems. For some systems, longer therapy sessions may also be more helpful, especially when doing trauma work.

◆ Having supervision with a therapist who also works/has worked with people with DID and OSDD can be helpful.

What Can Be Done to Help Prevent Future Childhood Trauma?
Trauma Education

◆ Education about trauma is important. People need to become more trauma aware and trauma-informed, whether this is parents, family or within education like schools or nurseries (preschool).

◆ Teach children how to ask for help. Let them know it is ok to ask for help. Let them know who they can go to if they need help or want to speak about something that has happened.

♦ Have regular conversations with children. Let them know that they can trust you as a parent or guardian and that they can tell you anything. Use the correct terminology for human sexual organs and anatomy and explain that no one else should ever touch their private parts and that their body is theirs only.

♦ Start conversations with people in your life about trauma and multiplicity to help educate others.

Schools

♦ Background checks (such as DBS checks in the UK) are an important preventative step in ensuring people with criminal records do not work with vulnerable people such as children. However, not all abusers have a criminal record.
♦ Offer support in schools, such as having school counsellors or mentors. The provision of breakfast clubs and after school clubs as a safe environment. Schools need to be aware of more vulnerable children.
♦ If schools are aware a child has experienced trauma, offering support to these children.
♦ Provide a safe and caring home and school environment.

Awareness and Support

♦ There are sometimes signs that children were/are going through something traumatic. Signs of physical abuse may be the easiest to spot. Be aware of this.
♦ Make sure you know what to do if you see signs of abuse or suspect abuse is happening. Know who to turn to and make

sure you keep this child safe. Know how to report the abuse and who to report it to.

+ Have accessible support for those who have experienced childhood trauma.

Change

+ Encourage children to speak about their feelings. If a child feels sad, comfort and support them. Let them know that it is ok to feel sad or angry. It is not bad.

+ Reduce the likelihood of ACEs. Trauma can be a political issue. Financial stability and access to free healthcare can help reduce trauma. A healthy family can better support traumatised children.

+ Change the rhetoric on how we speak about trauma. Ensuring the blame is never on the victim. Instead of asking 'What is wrong with you?' ask 'What happened to you?'

Conclusion

The brain is a complex and beautiful organ that has always been rooting for you. It stepped in during a time of crisis and gave you the gift of alters and amnesia to ensure your survival. The ultimate protection, the antidote to trauma, the creation of others to help you cope.

You survived trauma and you have the ability to recover from it too. You belong to a large community worldwide, who will always understand and who are on the same journey as you.

Systems deserve to be seen, heard, believed, accurately represented, understood, supported and loved. Slowly but surely, things are changing for the better and we can all be a part of this change. Let it be led by compassion, fuelled by knowledge and rooted in kindness, so that ignorance gives way to understanding.

The multiple mind may even reflect the universe itself. Some suggest it holds answers to the very fabric of existence. In the article 'Could multiple personality disorder explain life, the universe and everything?'[1] the idea is explored that, like DID, the universe itself could be one consciousness and that 'we may all be alters—dissociated personalities—of universal consciousness'.

DID and OSDD Dictionary of Terminology

Abuse – purposefully harming a person or animal.

Alter – a distinct, dissociated part of a person's identity in someone with DID, OSDD or P-DID. Alters have their own thoughts, emotions, memories, preferences and ways of perceiving the world. The term 'part' is also used to describe the same phenomenon.

Anxiety – feeling worried or fearful.

Blended – when two or more alters are mixed together, so they do not feel like their fully separate selves. Instead, they may feel like a single, combined experience or presence. Blending is different from co-consciousness, where there is dual (or multiple) awareness of separate identities at the same time.

Co-consciousness – when two or more alters are aware of each other and experiencing the present at the same time.

Comorbid disorder – having more than one disorder, diagnosis or mental health condition at the same time. For example, a person with DID might also have depression and OCD.

Crisis – a mental health crisis is when life becomes too overwhelming to cope with, making the person more vulnerable to factors such as self-harm, suicide and risky behaviours.

DDNOS – dissociative disorder not otherwise specified. This is an older term and has mostly been replaced by OSDD.

Depersonalisation – feeling detached from yourself, as if you are not real or are observing yourself from outside your body.

Depression – feeling intense sadness and a loss of motivation and interest in life. Not being able to experience happiness.

Derealisation – feeling as though the world around you is unreal, distant or dreamlike.

DID – dissociative identity disorder.

Dissociation – detaching from the present moment, floating away from reality or zoning out.

Dissociative amnesia – difficulty recalling important personal information, memories or parts of your past, beyond ordinary forgetfulness.

DSM – The Diagnostic and Statistical Manual of Mental Disorders. It is the handbook used by healthcare professionals in the United States and much of the world as the authoritative guide to the diagnosis of mental disorders.

Fakeclaiming – when people wrongly accuse a system of faking the condition. This is a discriminatory thing to say. It is harmful and invalidating.

'Final' fusion – the term used to describe one possible recovery outcome for systems. It describes the process in which all alters integrate and merge (fuse) to become one identity.

Flashback – when someone experiences a memory from their past, reliving it as if it is happening right now in the present moment. Flashbacks can be of trauma.

Fronting – when an alter is present in awareness and is in control of the body.

Frontstuck – when an alter stays in control (fronting) for a long time without switching. The alter may feel stuck or very tired.

Functional multiplicity – the term used to describe one possible recovery outcome for systems. It describes the process in which all alters learn to function effectively together while remaining multiple.

Fusion – when two (or more) alters merge and function as one, with the amnesic barriers between them breaking down.

Grounding – a technique that helps you stay in the present moment. It can be helpful in many situations, such as after dissociating or experiencing flashbacks. Examples include feeling your feet on the floor, holding something cold or noticing the sounds around you.

Highway hypnosis – when a driver goes on autopilot while driving and does not remember the journey. It is a form of dissociation.

Hypervigilance – is when the nervous system is on high alert, being hyper aware and always on the lookout for threat or danger. It is often a response to having trauma.

ICD-11 – International Classification of Diseases, 11th Revision. It is the global standard for diagnostic health information created by the World Health Organization (WHO), including mental health diagnoses.

Inner world – an internal space in the mind where alters can exist, interact or retreat when they are not fronting.

Inpatient – someone can be an inpatient in both a general and psychiatric hospital. Being an inpatient means that you are a patient who is staying the night in a hospital. One can be an inpatient for one night or up to weeks, months and, in a few cases, years.

Multiple – a person who has DID, OSDD or P-DID, meaning they have multiple alters in one body.

Multiple personality disorder – the old diagnostic name for dissociative identity disorder.

Multiplicity – also known as plurality is the presence of multiple dissociated identities (known as alters or parts) within one person.

Neurodivergent – neurodivergent means that your brain works differently to what may be considered 'typical'. People with conditions such as autism, ADHD and dyslexia are a key part of a balanced, neurodiverse society. People with DID and OSDD are also considered neurodiverse.[1]

Neurodiversity – the term neurodiversity is used to explain the concept that our brains all work differently. Neurodiversity celebrates the value that our different strengths can bring to the world. It isn't a new concept – neurodiversity has always existed in every society. It's just been given a name now.[2]

Neurotypical – neurotypical refers to someone whose brain falls within the societal standards of what is considered 'typical'.[3]

Non-system – a person who does not have DID, OSDD or P-DID and who experiences themselves as a single continuous identity (also known as a singlet).

OSDD – other specified dissociative disorder.

Part – a distinct, dissociated aspect of a person's identity in someone with DID, OSDD or P-DID. Parts have their own thoughts, emotions, memories, preferences and ways of perceiving the world. The term 'alter' is also used to describe the same phenomenon. The word 'part' is also used in Internal Family Systems (IFS) therapy to describe aspects of identity in people who do not have DID or OSDD. These IFS parts are not the same as the dissociated parts/alters seen in DID or OSDD.

Partner system – a system who is in a relationship with another system or an alter in that system. The relationship is not always romantic, it can be platonic.

Polyfragmented systems – refers to a system that has a large number of alters (often over 100) and/or many fragments or subsystems.

Polyvagal Theory – a theory proposed by Stephen Porges based on the role of the vagus nerve and the evolution of the parasympathetic and sympathetic nervous system. It explores how humans respond and adapt to danger or trauma.[4]

Programmed systems – a system that was deliberately traumatised and manipulated through mind control techniques to create dissociation and multipliclity. Programming is a form of abuse and torture.

Pronouns – pronouns are the way in which one refers to others such as he/him, she/her and they/them. Systems may refer to themselves as 'we'. This is them referring to their system as a whole.

Psychiatric hospital – a hospital for people with mental health conditions. The hospital can include both inpatient and outpatient settings.

Self-harm – when someone or an alter deliberately harms themselves. This could be physically or psychologically.

Singlet – a person who does not have DID, OSDD or P-DID and who experiences themselves as a single, continuous identity (also known as non-system).

Split – a psychological horror-thriller film about a man with DID who commits horrific crimes. The film is widely criticised for its inaccurate and stigmatising portrayal of DID.

Subsystems – systems within a DID or OSDD system.

Switch – the process of changing from one alter to another.

System – the collective term for all the alters/parts in one body (e.g. 'I'm an alter in this system').

System meeting – an organised meeting between two or more alters to discuss important issues regarding their system.

Trauma – a distressing, overwhelming or frightening experience that overwhelms a person's ability to cope and affects their mental and emotional health.

Unblending – refers to the process of separating alters who may be blended together while fronting. It allows you to observe and support another alter's emotions without being overwhelmed by them.

Recommended Resources

The following selection of organisations, resources and tools may be helpful for people with DID, OSDD, P-DID and their supporters. Inclusion does not imply endorsement and availability may vary by region.

Recommended Reading

Baer, R. (2007) *Switching Time: A Doctor's Harrowing Story of Treating a Woman with 17 Personalities*. New York: Crown Publishing Group.

Brand, B.L., Lanius, R.A. and Schielke, H.J. (2022) *The Finding Solid Ground Program Workbook: Overcoming Obstacles in Trauma Recovery*. Oxford: Oxford University Press.

Boon, S., Steele, K. and Van Der Hart, O. (2011) *Coping with Trauma-Related Dissociation: Skills Training for Patients and Therapists*. New York City: W.W. Norton & Company.

Chase, O. (2011) *The Sum of My Parts: A Survivor's Story of Dissociative Identity Disorder*. New York: Penguin Group.

Clark, J.D. (2019) *The Patchwork Quilt: A Book for Children about Dissociative Identity Disorder (DID)*. United States of America: Kindle Direct Publishing.

Emezi, A. (2018) *Freshwater*. London: Faber & Faber.

Fisher, J. (2017) *Healing the Fragmented Selves of Trauma Survivors*. New York: Routledge.

Fisher, J. (2021) *Transforming the Living Legacy of Trauma: A Workbook for Survivors and Therapists*. Wisconsin: PESI Publishing & Media. (This book is especially helpful for those who are currently not in therapy, allowing systems to do some self-work. It is not a replacement for therapy but a helpful tool.)

Frost, G. (2023) *The Girls Within: A True Story of Triumph Over Trauma and Abuse Gill Frost*. London: Phoenix Publishing House.

González, A. (2020) *It Is Not Me: Understanding and Healing Dissociative Disorders*. Barcelona: Desclée De Brouwer.

Haddock, D.B. (2001) *The Dissociative Identity Disorder Sourcebook.* New York: McGraw-Hill Education.

Harris, B.N. (2001) *The Deepest Well: Healing the Long-term Effects of Childhood Adversity.* Boston, MA: Houghton Mifflin Harcourt.

Herschel-Shorland, C. and Schofield, L. (2021) *Our House: Making Sense of Dissociative Identity Disorder.* New York: Routledge.

Howell, E.F. (2011) *Understanding and Treating Dissociative Identity Disorder: A Relational Approach.* New York: Routledge.

International Society for the Study of Trauma and Dissociation: *Journal of Trauma & Dissociation.* (The official scientific journal of the International Society for the Study of Trauma and Dissociation.)

Jamieson, A. (2009) *Today I Am Alice: Nine Personalities, One Tortured Mind.* London: Hodder & Stoughton.

Kastrup, B., Crabtree, A. and Kelly, E.F. (2018) 'Could multiple personality disorder explain life, the universe and everything?' *Scientific American.* Available at: https://url.de.m.mimecastprotect.com/s/UnbGCEqJXnClm667HZtZT7BrJe?domain=scientificamerican.com

Knyn, J. (2025) *My Mommy Has Multiple Parts: A children's book about having a parent with Dissociative Identity Disorder.* Guided Healing Psychology.

Marich, J. (2023) *Dissociation Made Simple: A Stigma-Free Guide to Embracing Your Dissociative Mind and Navigating Daily Life.* Berkeley, CA: North Atlantic Books.

Maté, D. and Maté, G. (2022) *The Myth of Normal: Trauma, Illness and Healing in a Toxic Culture.* London: Ebury Publishing.

Maté, G. (2019) *When the Body Says No: The Cost of Hidden Stress.* London: Penguin Random House.

McKernan, L. (2017) *The Tribe: Living and Healing from Dissociative Identity Disorder.* London: Jessica Kingsley Publishers.

Menakem, R. (2021) *My Grandmother's Hands: Racialized Trauma and the Pathway to Mending Our Hearts and Bodies.* London: Penguin Books Limited.

Miller, J. (2008) *Telling Without Talking: Art as a Window into the World of Multiple Personality.* London: Jessica Kingsley Publishers.

Miller, J. (2016) *Dear Little Ones: A Book for Children Who Have Experienced Trauma.* CreateSpace Independent Publishing Platform.

Minton, K., Ogden, P. and Pain, C. (2006) *Trauma and the Body: A Sensorimotor Approach to Psychotherapy.* New York: W.W. Norton & Company.

Nijenhuis, E.R.S., Steele, K. and Van Der Hart, O. (2006) *The Haunted Self: Structural Dissociation and the Treatment of Chronic Traumatization.* New York: W.W. Norton & Company.

Noble, K. (2011) *All of Me: How I Learned to Live with the Many Personalities Sharing My Body.* London: Piatkus.

Ogden, P. and Fisher, J. (2014) *Sensorimotor Psychotherapy: Interventions for Trauma and Attachment.* New York: W.W. Norton & Company.

O'Neill, J. (2018) *The Girl in the Green Dress.* London: Mirror Books.

Oxnam, R.B. (2005) *A Fractured Mind: My Life with Multiple Personality Disorder.* New York: Hyperion.

Pattillo, C. (2012) I Am We: My Life with Multiple Personalities. Bloomington: AuthorHouse.

Popelka, M. (2022) *You're Going to Be Okay: 16 Lessons on Healing After Trauma.* London: Hay House.

Ross, C.A. (1997) *Living with the Reality of Dissociative Identity Disorder: Campaigning for Change.* Richardson: Manitou Communications.

Ruff, M. (2003) *Set This House in Order: A Romance of Souls.* London: Harper Perennial.

Sarson, M. (2017) *Scared Selfless: My Journey from Abuse and Madness to Surviving and Thriving.* New York: William Morrow.

Schnall, M. and Steinberg, M. (2000) *The Stranger in the Mirror: Dissociation—The Hidden Epidemic.* New York: HarperCollins.

Schwartz, T. and Galperin, B. (2000) *Amongst Ourselves: A Self-Help Guide to Living with Dissociative Identity Disorder.* Oakland: New Harbinger Publications.

Siegel, D.J. and Solomon, M.F. (2003) *Healing Trauma: Attachment, Mind, Body and Brain.* New York: W.W. Norton & Company.

Spring, C. (2014) *Recovery Is My Best Revenge.* Huntingdon: Carolyn Spring Publishing.

Spring, C. (2018) *Unshame: Healing Trauma-Based Shame Through Psychotherapy.* Cambridge: Carolyn Spring.

The Troops for Truddi Chase (1990) *When Rabbit Howls.* New York: Berkley Books.

Tohid, H. and Rutkofsky, I.H. (2023) *Dissociative Identity Disorder: Treatment and Management.* New York: Springer.

Van Der Kolk, B. (2014) *The Body Keeps the Score: Brain, Mind, and Body in the Healing of Trauma.* New York: Viking Press.

Walker, H. (2008) *Breaking Free: My Life with Dissociative Identity Disorder.* New York: Simon & Schuster.

Walker, R. (2020) *The Unapologetic Guide to Black Mental Health: Navigate an Unequal System, Learn Tools for Emotional Wellness, and Get the Help You Deserve.* Oakland, CA: New Harbinger Publications.

Wasnak, L. (2000) *Mending Ourselves: Expressions of Healing & Self-Discovery.* New York: Writers Club Press.

Wegscheider, J. (1996) *I Am More Than One: How Women with Dissociative Identity Disorder Have Found Success in Life and Work.* New York: HarperCollins.

Zweig, S. (2006) *Chess Story.* London: Penguin Classics. (Note: Originally published in 1942 as 'Schachnovelle'.)

Journals and Tools

CBT Skills Cards. Available at: https://dissociationinfo.etsy.com/listing/1671482420

DBT Skills Cards. Available at: https://dissociationinfo.etsy.com/listing/1473445594

DID and OSDD Crisis Cards. Available at: https://dissociationinfo.etsy.com/listing/1179765879

Grounding Cards. Available at: https://dissociationinfo.etsy.com/listing/1234810286

Mindfulness Cards. Available at: https://dissociationinfo.etsy.com/listing/1791526291

The DID & OSDD Journal. Available as a PDF from at: www.etsy.com/uk/listing/1494667804/the-ultimate-did-osdd-journal-workbook?etsrc=sdt and as a physical book from Amazon.

International Organisations and Resources

A Couple of Multiples is a podcast run by two systems which raises awareness about dissociative identity disorder. It is for people with DID, supporters and clinicians. www.acoupleofmultiples.com

An Infinite Mind is an international grass-roots non-profit organisation that provides direct education, advocacy and support services to people living with dissociative disorders. www.aninfinitemind.org

Carolyn Spring is an advocate for DID and a professional by experience. There are lots of excellent blog posts on her website covering a variety of topics about living as a system. www.carolynspring.com

DissociationInfo (Etsy) is a shop by the author of this book, offering mental health resources, including those specifically designed for people with DID and OSDD. www.etsy.com/uk/shop/DissociationInfo

@Dissociation.info (Instagram) is a supportive and educational community sharing lived experiences and posts about DID, OSDD, and trauma.

Healing My Parts Podcast is a podcast about dissociative identity disorder and trauma: a therapist's personal journey of healing and discovery, which aims to empower people with DID and the professionals who support them. https://healingmyparts.substack.com/podcast

International Society for the Study of Trauma and Dissociation (ISSTD) is a non-profit professional association which seeks to advance clinical, scientific, and societal understanding of chronic trauma dissociative disorders. The ISSTD offers specialised training and events. The ISSTD has a therapist directory on their website. https://isstdworld.isst-d.org/network/network-find-a-professional

The Institute for Creative Mindfulness is an organisation offering educational resources, training and certification programmes. They have a key focus on mindfulness practices, EMDR and creative therapies to help support people dealing with trauma, stress and anxiety. www.institutefor creativemindfulness.com

Many Voices Magazine was a magazine offering words of hope for people recovering from trauma and dissociation. All issues of Many Voices from 1989 to 2012 are available to read online or download as PDFs. www.manyvoicespress.org/newsletter.html

Multiplied By One Org is a charity for complex trauma, dissociative disorders and loved ones. Their international services include online support groups, a magazine, resources, the Pocket Advocate app and a therapist directory. https://directory.multipliedbyone.org/therapist

Nscience offers professional development and training for therapists through seminars, workshops, conferences and online courses. Their training includes understanding and working with childhood trauma and dissociative disorders. www.nscience.uk

PESI (US/UK/Canada/Australia) offers training for psychotherapists, counsellors, psychologists and mental health professionals. Including courses on dissociative disorders and trauma. www.pesi.co.uk, www.pesi.com

Simply Plural is an app to help systems keep track of their members.

System Speak is a podcast run by a DID system that documents their healing journey and their thoughts on DID, dissociation trauma and mental health. www.systemspeakpodcast.com

The Plural Association is a 'by plurals, for plurals' non-profit international organisation founded in the Netherlands. www.powertotheplurals.com

UK Organisations

Beacon House offers a specialist adult complex trauma and dissociative disorders clinic where they assess and treat dissociative disorders. www.beaconhouse.org.uk

BEAT is a charity supporting people with eating disorders. www.beateating disorders.org.uk

The Black, African and Asian Therapy Network is the largest community of Counsellors and Psychotherapists of Black, African, Asian and Caribbean Heritage in the UK. www.baatn.org.uk

The British Association of Art Therapists is the professional membership organisation for art therapists in the UK. They have an online art therapist finder tool on their website. https://baat.org/find-an-art-therapist

The British Association for Counselling and Psychotherapy (BACP) is the professional association for members of the counselling professions in the UK. They have a therapist directory on their website. www.bacp.co.uk/search/Therapists

CALM (Campaign Against Living Miserably) is a charity leading a movement against suicide. If you are struggling with suicidal thoughts they have a help line number you can call, a WhatsApp number you can message and an online live chat. www.thecalmzone.net

CDS UK (Clinic for Dissociative Studies) is a charity supporting children and adults who have dissociative disorders and complex trauma. They offer assessments and psychotherapy in various locations across England and accept referrals from the NHS. www.clinicds.org.uk

Citizens Advice is a charity in the UK that offers free advice in many areas such as benefits, work, debt and money, housing, law and courts, immigration and health. www.citizensadvice.org.uk

Cruse Bereavement Support is a charity in the UK that has a helpline for grief support: 0808 808 1677 www.cruse.org.uk

CTAD Clinic offers private psychotherapy and assessments for dissociative disorders. www.cheshirepsychology.com

DBTSelfHelp.com is a DBT self-help website recommended by Mind. https://dbtselfhelp.com

The Dissociative Disorders Alliance (The DDA) is the UK's national charity aiming to improve quality of life and outcomes for people with complex dissociative disorders. www.thedissociativedisordersalliance.org.uk

MentalHealthUK is a charity that provides crucial advice, information and support to those affected by mental health problems. www.mentalhealth-uk.org

Mind is a mental health charity that offers help through their award-winning information online, advice and local services. Over 100 local Minds across England and Wales run mental health services in local communities. Mind campaigns to improve services, raise awareness and promote understanding. Their legal line offers legal information and general advice on mental health related law: 0300 466 6463. Their support line is a safe space for you to talk about your mental health: 0300 102 1234. www.mind.org.uk

The Mix is the UK's leading support service for young people. They offer help with mental health, money, homelessness, finding a job, break-ups, drugs and more. www.themix.org.uk

My Body Back is a volunteer-run organisation; they work with the NHS to offer special clinics for people who've experienced sexual violence. This includes cervical screening, contraceptive care, STI testing and maternity care. https://mybodybackproject.com

National Association for People Abused in Childhood (NAPAC) is a charity in the UK that offers support to adult survivors of all types of childhood abuse. Helpline: 0808 801 0331, support@napac.org.uk, www.napac.org.uk

National Health Service (NHS) CBT Techniques offers practical self-help tips and strategies. www.nhs.uk/every-mind-matters/mental-wellbeing-tips/self-help-cbt-techniques

Nightline Association is a student-run charity listening and information service, open at night when other services on campus may be closed. www.nightline.org.uk

Patient Advice and Liaison Service (PALS) NHS UK offers advice and support and is where you can send complaints and concerns regarding your/someone's care in the NHS. This includes psychiatric hospitals and mental health services. www.nhs.uk/nhs-services/hospitals/what-is-pals-patient-advice-and-liaison-service

Pink Therapy is the UK's largest independent therapy organisation working with gender, sex or relationship diverse clients. The website includes a therapist directory. https://pinktherapy.com

The Pottergate Centre for Trauma and Dissociation offers private psychotherapy and assessments for dissociative disorders. www.dissociation.co.uk

Rethink is a charity in England that offers mental health services, support groups and mental health training. www.rethink.org

Samaritans is a charity in the UK that has a free helpline for when you are in crisis or need someone to talk to: call 116 123 or email jo@samaritans.org. www.samaritans.org

Sane is a mental health charity in the UK. www.sane.org.uk

Shout is a text support service: text 85258. https://giveusashout.org

The Stay Alive app is a pocket suicide prevention resource for the UK, which can include your safety plan, a life box for photos that are special to you and a place to write reasons for living.

The Survivors Trust is the largest umbrella agency for specialist rape and sexual abuse services in the UK. www.thesurvivorstrust.org

The UK Council for Psychotherapy (UKCP) is the leading organisation for psychotherapists and psychotherapeutic counsellors in the UK. They have a therapist directory on their website. www.psychotherapy.org.uk/find-a-therapist

Victim Support is a charity in England and Wales that offers support to victims of crime and traumatic incidents. www.victimsupport.org.uk

VoiceAbility is a charity providing advocacy and involvement services regarding health, care and wellbeing, including mental healthcare. www.voiceability.org.

YoungMinds is a charity fighting for children and young people's mental health. www.youngminds.org

Other European Organisations and Resources

Caleidoscoop is the national association for people with a dissociative disorder in the Netherlands. www.caleidoscoop.nl

Suomen trauma- ja dissosiaatioyhdistys Disso ry/Finnish Trauma and Dissociation Association produces and shares information on psychological traumatisation and dissociation, and develops various peer support methods. www.disso.fi

The European Society for Trauma and Dissociation (ESTD) supports research and the development of knowledge about clinical effects of complex trauma, recognition of symptoms, proper diagnosis and treatment of trauma-related disorders. They support collaboration between scientists and clinicians from around the world, conducting webinars and training with experts in the field, and organising international congresses. The ESTD has a therapist directory on their website. https://estd.org

USA and Canada Organisations and Resources

211 is a comprehensive source of information about local resources and services. Call this number to get help with mental health, housing, bills and food. www.211.org

Beauty After Bruises is a project helping adult survivors of childhood trauma who have Complex PTSD and/or dissociative trauma disorders. www.beautyafterbruises.org

Canadian Mental Health Association (CMHA) is the most established, most extensive community mental health organisation in Canada. https://cmha.ca

The Child-Help USA This crisis line (1 800 422 4453) assists child and adult survivors of abuse, including sexual abuse. It is staffed by mental health professionals and provides treatment referrals. www.childhelp.org

Crisis Services Canada. The Canada Suicide Prevention Service: call 1 833 456 4566 or text 45645. www.canada.ca/en/public-health/services/mental-health-services/mental-health-get-help.html

Crisis Text Line. Text HOME to 741741 to speak with a trained crisis counsellor (USA and Canada). www.crisistextline.org

Dr Adrian Fletcher. See www.drfletch.com and article 'Multilayered' published by the American Psychiatric Association: https://ps.psychiatryonline.org/doi/10.1176/appi.ps.202100706

Kids Help Phone is Canada's only 24/7 e-mental health service offering free, confidential support to young people in English and French. Text with a crisis responder, text CONNECT to 686868 or call 1 800 668 6868.

Mental Health America (MHA) is the United States' leading community-based non-profit dedicated to addressing the needs of those living with mental illness and promoting the overall mental health of all. www.mhanational.org

NAMI (the National Alliance on Mental Illness) provides advocacy, education, support and public awareness. www.nami.org

The National Child Traumatic Stress Network was created by Congress in 2000 as part of the Children's Health Act to raise the standard of care and increase access to services for children and families who experience or witness traumatic events. www.nctsn.org

National Suicide Prevention Lifeline is a helpline in the United States open 24 hours a day and 7 days a week: 1 800 273 8255 or 988.

Rape Abuse and Incest National Network (RAINN) is the nation's largest anti-sexual violence organisation. National Sexual Assault Hotline: Call 800 656 HOPE (4673).

Sidran Traumatic Stress Institute is a non-profit organisation that helps people understand, recover from and treat PTSD and dissociative disorders. www.traumaticstressinstitute.org/sidran-redirect

Substance Abuse and Mental Health Services Administration (SAMHSA) has a national helpline (1 800 662 HELP (4357)) and can make referrals to local treatment facilities, support groups and community-based organisations. www.samhsa.gov

U.S. Department of Health and Human Services lists free clinics in your location. www.hhs.gov

Australia and New Zealand Organisations and Resources

Beyond Blue is Australia's most well-known and visited mental health organisation. www.beyondblue.org.au

Blue Knot Foundation is an Australian organisation that provides information and support to anyone who is affected by complex trauma. www.blueknot.org.au

Lifeline (Australia). Call 13 11 14, text 0477 13 11 14.

Lifeline (New Zealand). Call 0800 543 354, text HELP (4357).

The Mental Health Foundation of New Zealand is a mental health charity. www.mentalhealth.org.nz

References

Chapter 1

1   American Psychiatric Association (1994) *Diagnostic and Statistical Manual of Mental Disorders, 4th edition (DSM-IV)*. Arlington, VA: APA.
2   American Psychiatric Association (2013) *Diagnostic and Statistical Manual of Mental Disorders, 5th edition (DSM-5)*. Arlington, VA: APA.
3   World Health Organization (2025) 'Dissociative identity disorder (6B64)', *International Classification of Diseases 11th Revision (ICD-11)*. Accessed on 14/02/25 at: https://icd.who.int/browse/2025-01/mms/en#1829103493
4   Dell, P. and O'Neil, J. (2011, first published 2009) *Dissociation and the Dissociative Disorders: DSM-V and Beyond*. New York: Routledge, p.694.
5   World Health Organization (2025) 'Partial dissociative identity disorder (6B65)', *International Classification of Diseases 11th Revision (ICD-11)*. Accessed on 21/06/2025 at: https://icd.who.int/browse/2025-01/mms/en#988400777
6   International Society for the Study of Trauma and Dissociation (2011) 'Guidelines for Treating Dissociative Identity Disorder in Adults: PHASE-ORIENTED TREATMENT APPROACH and EPIDEMIOLOGY, CLINICAL DIAGNOSIS, AND DIAGNOSTIC PROCEDURES.' *Journal of Trauma & Dissociation, Third Revision*, 12:2, p.118. Accessed on 21/04/22 at: www.isst-d.org/wp-content/uploads/2019/02/GUIDELINES_REVISED2011.pdf
7   American Psychiatric Association (2013) 'Dissociative Disorders, Dissociative Identity Disorder, Prevalence', in *Diagnostic and Statistical Manual of Mental Disorders* (5th edn). Arlington, VA: American Psychiatric Association, p.294.
8   American Psychiatric Association (2013) 'Obsessive-Compulsive Disorder, Prevalence', in *Diagnostic and Statistical Manual of Mental Disorders* (5th edn). Arlington, VA: American Psychiatric Association, p.239.
9   American Psychiatric Association (2013) 'Schizophrenia Spectrum and Other Psychotic Disorders, Prevalence', in *Diagnostic and Statistical Manual of Mental Disorders* (5th edn). Arlington, VA: American Psychiatric Association, p.102.
10 Reinders, A.A.T.S. and Veltman, D.J. (2021) 'Dissociative identity disorder: Out of the shadows at last?' *The British Journal of Psychiatry 210*, 413. Accessed on 09/02/25 at: www.cambridge.org/core/services/aop-cambridge-core/content/view/8E2884FA8669A9A64790E5C47AD72DC7/S0007125020001683a.pdf/dissociative-identity-disorder-out-of-the-shadows-at-last.pdf

11 United Nations Population Fund (2022) 'Foreword.' *State of World Population 2023: 8 Billion Lives, Infinite Possibilities – The Case for Rights and Choices*, United Nations Population Fund, p.4. Accessed on 18/04/25 at: www.unfpa.org/sites/default/files/swop23/SWOP2023-ENGLISH-230329-web.pdf

12 Kate, M.A., Hopwood, T. and Jamieson, G. (2019) 'The prevalence of dissociative disorders and dissociative experiences in college populations: A meta-analysis of 98 studies.' *Journal of Trauma & Dissociation 21*, 1, 16–61. Accessed on 14/02/25 at: www.tandfonline.com/doi/full/10.1080/15299732.2019.1647915

13 Tohid, H. and Rutkofsky, I.H. (2023) 'Dissociative Identity Disorder and Other Specified Dissociative Disorder (OSDD).' *Dissociative Identity Disorder: Treatment and Management*. New York: Springer, p.87.

14 Tohid, H. and Rutkofsky, I.H. (2023) 'Dissociative Identity Disorder and Other Specified Dissociative Disorder (OSDD).' *Dissociative Identity Disorder: Treatment and Management*. New York: Springer, p.87.

15 Tohid, H. and Rutkofsky, I.H. (2023) 'History of Dissociative Identity Disorder (DID).' *Dissociative Identity Disorder: Treatment and Management*. New York: Springer, p.4.

16 Centers for Disease Control and Prevention (CDC) (2024) *About Child Sexual Abuse*. Accessed on 18/02/25 at: www.cdc.gov/child-abuse-neglect/about/about-child-sexual-abuse.html?CDC_AAref_Val=https://www.cdc.gov/violenceprevention/childsexualabuse/fastfact.html#cdc_behavioral_basics_quick-quick-facts-and-stats

17 Loewenstein, R.J. (2018) 'Dissociation debates: Everything you know is wrong.' *Dialogues in Clinical Neuroscience 20*, 3, 229–242. Accessed on 31/05/22 at: https://doi.org/10.31887/DCNS.2018.20.3/rloewenstein

18 Tohid, H. and Rutkofsky, I.H. (2023) 'History of Dissociative Identity Disorder (DID).' *Dissociative Identity Disorder: Treatment and Management*. New York: Springer, p.1.

19 Brand, B.L., Şar, V., and Shane, E. (2016) 'Separating fact from fiction: An empirical examination of six myths about dissociative identity disorder.' *Harvard Review of Psychiatry 24*, 4, 257–270. Accessed on 16/02/25 at: https://journals.lww.com/hrpjournal/fulltext/2016/07000/separating_fact_from_fiction__an_empirical.2.aspx

Chapter 2

1 Department of Health and Social Care (2021) 'UK Rare Diseases Framework. Introduction.' Accessed on 01/08/25 at: https://www.gov.uk/government/publications/uk-rare-diseases-framework/the-uk-rare-diseases-framework

2 Reinders, A.A.T.S., Willemsen, A.T.M., Vos, H.P.J., den Boer, J.A. and Nijenhuis, E.R.S. (2012) 'Fact or factitious? A psychobiological study of authentic and simulated dissociative identity states' *PLOS ONE 7*, 6, e39279. Accessed on 02/07/25 at: https://journals.plos.org/plosone/article?id=10.1371/journal.pone.0039279

3 American Psychiatric Association (2013) 'Dissociative Disorders, Dissociative Identity Disorder, Prevalence', in *Diagnostic and Statistical Manual of Mental Disorders* (5th edn). Arlington, VA: American Psychiatric Association, p.294.

4   United Nations Population Fund (2022) 'Foreword.' *State of World Population 2023: 8 Billion Lives, Infinite Possibilities – The Case for Rights and Choices*, United Nations Population Fund, p.4. Accessed on 18/04/25 at: www.unfpa.org/sites/default/files/swop23/SWOP2023-ENGLISH-230329-web.pdf

5   King's College London Institute of Psychiatry, Psychology & Neuroscience, Victim Support, Mind, *et al.* (2013) 'People with mental health problems at high risk of being victims of crime'. King's College London Archive. Accessed on 10/07/25 at: www.kcl.ac.uk/archive/news/ioppn/records/2013/october/people-with-mental-health-problems-at-high-risk-of-being-victims-of-crime

6   Tohid, H. and Rutkofsky, I.H. (2023) 'Dissociative Identity Disorder: Theory vs. Facts.' *Dissociative Identity Disorder: Treatment and Management*. New York: Springer, p.17.

7   Shyamalan, M. (2016) *Split*. Blinding Edge Pictures, Blumhouse Productions, Universal Pictures.

8   International Society for the Study of Trauma and Dissociation (2011) 'Guidelines for treating Dissociative Identity Disorder in adults: Phase-oriented treatment approach and epidemiology, clinical diagnosis, and diagnostic procedures.' *Journal of Trauma & Dissociation, Third Revision* 12, 2, 118. Accessed on 21/04/22 at www.isst-d.org/wp-content/uploads/2019/02/GUIDELINES_REVISED2011.pdf

9   Brand, B.L., Şar, V. and Shane, E. (2016) 'Separating fact from fiction: An empirical examination of six myths about dissociative identity disorder.' *Harvard Review of Psychiatry* 24, 4, 257–270. Accessed on 16/02/25 at: https://journals.lww.com/hrpjournal/fulltext/2016/07000/separating_fact_from_fiction__an_empirical.2.aspx

Chapter 3

1   Nijenhuis, E.R.S., Steele, K. and Van Der Hart, O. (2006) *The Haunted Self: Structural Dissociation and the Treatment of Chronic Traumatization*. New York: W.W. Norton & Company.

2   Loewenstein, R.J. (2018) 'Dissociation debates: Everything you know is wrong.' *Dialogues in Clinical Neuroscience* 20, 3, 229–242. Accessed on 31/05/22 at: https://doi.org/10.31887/DCNS.2018.20.3/rloewenstein

3   Hershler, A., Hughes, L., Nguyen, P. and Wall, S. (2021) 'Window of Tolerance.' *Looking at Trauma: A Tool Kit for Clinicians*. University Park, PA: The Pennsylvania State University Press.

4   Brand, B.L., Şar, V. and Shane, E. (2016) 'Separating fact from fiction: An empirical examination of six myths about dissociative identity disorder.' *Harvard Review of Psychiatry* 24, 4, 257–270. Accessed on 16/02/25 at: https://journals.lww.com/hrpjournal/fulltext/2016/07000/separating_fact_from_fiction__an_empirical.2.aspx

5   Brand, B.L., Dorahy, M.J., Krüger, C., Lewis-Fernández, R. *et al.* (2014) 'Dissociative identity disorder: An empirical overview.' *Australian and New Zealand Journal of Psychiatry* 48, 5, 402–412. Accessed on 25/05/22 at: www.researchgate.net/publication/262025048_Dissociative_identity_disorder_An_empirical_overview

6   Patel, R.S., Patel, T. and Araujo, J.F. 'Dissociative Identity Disorder: A Pathophysiological Phenomenon' *Journal of Psychiatric Research and Treatment 1*, 1, 1–7.

Accessed on 06/07/25 at: www.researchgate.net/publication/308905099_
Dissociative_Identity_Disorder_A_Pathophysiological_Phenomenon

7   Chalavi, S., Dazzan, P., Jäncke, L., Marquand, A. *et al.* (2019) 'Aiding the diag-
    nosis of dissociative identity disorder: A pattern recognition study of brain
    biomarkers.' *British Journal of Psychiatry 215*, 3, 536–544. Accessed on 22/04/25
    at: https://doi.org/10.1192/bjp.2018.255

8   Kings College London (2018) 'Computers can "spot the difference" between
    healthy brains and the brains of people with Dissociative Identity Disorder.'
    Accessed on 01/05/22 at: www.kcl.ac.uk/archive/news/ioppn/records/2018/
    december/computers-can-'spot-the-difference'-between-healthy-brains-and-
    the-brains-of-people-with-dissociative-identity-disorder

9   Reinders, A.A.T.S. and Veltman, D.J. (2021) 'Dissociative identity disorder: Out
    of the shadows at last?' *The British Journal of Psychiatry 219*, 2, 413–414. Accessed
    on 06/02/25 at: www.cambridge.org/core/journals/the-british-journal-of-
    psychiatry/article/dissociative-identity-disorder-out-of-the-shadows-at-last
    /8E2884FA8669A9A64790E5C47AD72DC7

10 Purcell, J.B., Brand, B., Browne, H.A., Chefetz, R.A. *et al.* (2024) 'Treatment
    of dissociative identity disorder: Leveraging neurobiology to optimize suc-
    cess.' *Expert Review of Neurotherapeutics 24*, 3, 273–289. Accessed on 16/02/25
    at: www.tandfonline.com/doi/full/10.1080/14737175.2024.2316153

11 Scharfe, E. (2017) 'Attachment Theory.' *Encyclopedia of Evolutionary Psy-
    chological Science.* Accessed on 25/05/22 at: www.researchgate.net/
    publication/314117326_Attachment_Theory

Chapter 4

1   Tohid, H. and Rutkofsky, I.H. (2023) 'Epidemiology of Dissociative Identity
    Disorder.' *Dissociative Identity Disorder: Treatment and Management.* New York:
    Springer, p.149.

2   Tohid, H. and Rutkofsky, I.H. (2023) 'Epidemiology of Dissociative Identity
    Disorder.' *Dissociative Identity Disorder: Treatment and Management.* New York:
    Springer, p.50.

3   Tohid, H. and Rutkofsky, I.H. (2023) 'Dissociative Identity Disorder and the
    Law and A Psychiatrist's Perspective on DID.' *Dissociative Identity Disorder:
    Treatment and Management.* New York: Springer, p.50, p.285.

4   Fisher, J. (2017) *Healing the Fragmented Selves of Trauma Survivors.* New York:
    Routledge.

5   Power to the Plurals (2019) 'Fragments.' Accessed on 12/01/25 at www.
    powertotheplurals.com/fragments-did101

Chapter 7

1   International Society for the Study of Trauma and Dissociation (2011) 'Guide-
    lines for treating Dissociative Identity Disorder in adults: Phase-oriented
    treatment approach and epidemiology, clinical diagnosis, and diagnostic
    procedures.' *Journal of Trauma & Dissociation, Third Revision 12*, 2, 118. Accessed
    on 21/04/22 at: www.isst-d.org/wp-content/uploads/2019/02/GUIDELINES_
    REVISED2011.pdf

2   Braun, B.G. (1986) *Treatment of Multiple Personality Disorder*. Washington, DC: American Psychiatric Press.

1   Brand, B.L., Dorahy, M.J., Krüger, C., Lewis-Fernández, R. *et al.* (2014) 'Dissociative identity disorder: An empirical overview.' *Australian and New Zealand Journal of Psychiatry 48*, 5, 402–412. Accessed on 25/05/22 at: www.researchgate.net/publication/262025048_Dissociative_identity_disorder_An_empirical_overview

Chapter 8

Chapter 9

1   Maxis. Wright, W. (2014) The Sims 4. Electronic Arts.

Chapter 14

1   Brand, B.L., Dorahy, M.J., Krüger, C., Lewis-Fernández, R. *et al.* (2014) 'Dissociative disorders: An overview of assessment, phenomenology, and treatment.' *The Australian and New Zealand Journal of Psychiatry 48*, 5, 406.

Chapter 16

1   Hu, Z., Kaminga, A.C., Yang, J., Liu, J. *et al.* (2021) 'Adverse childhood experiences and risk of cancer during adulthood: A systematic review and meta-analysis.' *Child Abuse & Neglect: The International Journal.* Accessed on 31/05/22 at: https://pubmed.ncbi.nlm.nih.gov/33971569

Chapter 17

1   Merriam Webster (2025) 'Intersectionality.' *Merriam-Webster.com Dictionary.* Accessed on 18/04/25 at: www.merriam-webster.com/dictionary/intersectionality.

2   Investing in Ethnicity (2021) 'An Ethnicity Allies Guide to Getting it Right.' Accessed on 07/05/25 at: https://investinginethnicity.org/wp-content/uploads/2021/08/Ally-Toolkit-2021-V2-3.pdf

Chapter 19

1   Docter, P. and Del Carmen, R. (2015) *Inside Out*. Pixar Animation Studios, Walt Disney Pictures.

2   Clark, J.D. (2019) *The Patchwork Quilt: A Book for Children about Dissociative Identity Disorder (DID)*. USA: Kindle Direct Publishing.

3   Knyn, J. (2022) *My Mommy Has Multiple Parts: A Children's Book about Having a Parent with Dissociative Identity Disorder*. USA: Independently published.

Chapter 20

1   Shyamalan, M. (2016) *Split*. Blinding Edge Pictures, Blumhouse Productions, Universal Pictures.

2   Brand, B., Boyer, S.M., Caplan, J.E., Nester, M.S. *et al.* (2024) 'It's not just a movie: Perceived impact of misportrayals of dissociative identity disorder in the media on self and treatment – Conclusions.' *European Journal of Trauma &*

Dissociation 8, 3. Accessed on 09/02/25 at: www.sciencedirect.com/science/article/abs/pii/S2468749924000528

3   Sanderson, P. (2018) *The Lives I Lead: My Multiple Personalities*. BBC Radio 1. Accessed on 09/05/25 at: www.youtube.com/watch?v=exLDx09_ta8

4   Kimbrough, J. (2010) *The Woman with 15 Personalities*. MagellanTV. Accessed on 09/05/25 at: www.youtube.com/watch?v=ojzZ4L2rmSY&t=360s

5   Crumpler, D. (2022) *Petals of a Rose*. Accessed on 04/04/25 at: www.dylancrumpler.com/petals-of-a-rose

6   Mierendorf, M. (1993) *Multiple Personality Disorder: The Search for Deadly Memories*. HBO.

7   Docter, P. and Del Carmen, R. (2015) *Inside Out*. Pixar Animation Studios, Walt Disney Pictures.

8   Erickson, D. (2022) *Severance: Season 1*. Red Hour Productions, Endeavor Content, Apple TV+.

9   People Magazine (2021) 'AnnaLynne McCord on Her Identity Disorder and Coping After Sexual Abuse: "I've Experienced Hell"'. Accessed on 20/05/22 at: www.people.com/tv/annalynne-mccord-on-her-identity-disorder-and-coping-after-sexual-abuse

10 Dissociadid (n.d.) YouTube channel. Available at: www.youtube.com/@DissociaDID

11 The Entropy System. (n.d.) YouTube channel. Available at: www.youtube.com/@TheEntropySystem

12 Walker, H., Brozek, G. and Maxfield, C. (2008) *Breaking Free: My Life with Dissociative Identity Disorder*. New York: Simon & Schuster.

13 MultiplicityAndMe (n.d.) YouTube channel. Available at: www.youtube.com/@MultiplicityAndMe

14 Navasky, M., O'Connor, K. and O'Boyle, M. (2023) *Joan Baez: I Am a Noise*. Mead Street Films, Magnolia Pictures.

15 Baer, R. (2007) *Switching Time: A Doctor's Harrowing Story of Treating a Woman with 17 Personalities*. New York: Crown Publishing Group.

16 Noble, K. Artist. Website. Available at: www.kimnobleartist.com

17 Chase, T. (1987) *When Rabbit Howls*. New York: E.P. Dutton.

Chapter 21

1   Clinic for Dissociative Studies (CDS). Available at: www.clinicds.co.uk

2   Beacon House, Sussex. Available at: www.beaconhouse.org.uk

3   The Pottergate Centre, Norwich. Available at: www.dissociation.co.uk

4   The CTAD Clinic, Cheshire Psychology. Available at: www.cheshirepsychology.com

5   The Dissociative Experiences Scale (DES-II). Available at: www.researchgate.net/publication/232515683_An_Update_on_the_Dissociative_Experiences_Scale

6   The Somatoform Dissociation Questionnaire (SDC-5/SDQ-20). Available at: www.enijenhuis.nl/sdq20

7   The International Society for the Study of Trauma and Dissociation (ISSTD). Available at: www.isst-d.org/resources

8   Multidimensional Inventory of Dissociation (MID). Available at: www.mid-assessment.com

9   Dissociative Disorders Interview Schedule (DDIS). Available at: www.rossinst. com/ddis

10 International Society for the Study of Trauma and Dissociation (2011) 'Guidelines for treating Dissociative Identity Disorder in adults: Phase-oriented treatment approach and epidemiology, clinical diagnosis, and diagnostic procedures.' *Journal of Trauma & Dissociation, Third Revision* 12, 2, 126. Accessed on 21/04/22 at: www.isst-d.org/wp-content/uploads/2019/02/GUIDELINES_REVISED2011.pdf

11 Loewenstein, R.J. (2018) 'Dissociation debates: Everything you know is wrong.' *Dialogues in Clinical Neuroscience* 20, 3, 229–242. Accessed on 31/05/22 at: https://doi.org/10.31887/DCNS.2018.20.3/rloewenstein

12 Reinders, A.A.T.S. and Veltman, D.J. (2021) 'Dissociative identity disorder: Out of the shadows at last?' *The British Journal of Psychiatry* 210, 413. Accessed on 09/02/25 at: www.cambridge.org/core/services/aop-cambridge-core/content/view/8E2884FA8669A9A64790E5C47AD72DC7/S0007125020001683a.pdf/dissociative-identity-disorder-out-of-the-shadows-at-last.pdf

13 Reinders, A.A.T.S. and Veltman, D.J. (2021) 'Dissociative identity disorder: Out of the shadows at last?' *The British Journal of Psychiatry* 210, 413. Accessed on 09/02/25 at: www.cambridge.org/core/services/aop-cambridge-core/content/view/8E2884FA8669A9A64790E5C47AD72DC7/S0007125020001683a.pdf/dissociative-identity-disorder-out-of-the-shadows-at-last.pdf

14 Reinders, A.A.T.S. and Veltman, D.J. (2021) 'Dissociative identity disorder: Out of the shadows at last?' *The British Journal of Psychiatry* 210, 413. Accessed on 09/02/25 at: www.cambridge.org/core/services/aop-cambridge-core/content/view/8E2884FA8669A9A64790E5C47AD72DC7/S0007125020001683a.pdf/dissociative-identity-disorder-out-of-the-shadows-at-last.pdf

15 Definition of disability under the Equality Act (2010) London: HMSO Accessed on 20/05/22 at: www.legislation.gov.uk/uksi/2011/1159/made

Chapter 22

1   Purcell, J.B., Brand, B., Browne, H.A., Chefetz, R.A. *et al.* (2024) 'Treatment of dissociative identity disorder: Leveraging neurobiology to optimize success.' *Expert Review of Neurotherapeutics* 24, 3, 273–289. Accessed on 16/02/25 at: www.tandfonline.com/doi/full/10.1080/14737175.2024.2316153

2   International Society for the Study of Trauma and Dissociation (2011) 'Guidelines for treating Dissociative Identity Disorder in adults: Phase-oriented treatment approach and epidemiology, clinical diagnosis, and diagnostic procedures.' *Journal of Trauma & Dissociation, Third Revision* 12, 2, 126. Accessed on 21/04/22 at: www.isst-d.org/wp-content/uploads/2019/02/GUIDELINES_REVISED2011.pdf

3   Sweezy, M. and Ziskind, E.L. (2013) *Internal Family Systems Therapy: New Dimensions.* New York: Routledge.

Chapter 23

1   Mental Health Act (1983) London: HMSO. Accessed on 13/05/22 at: www.legislation.gov.uk/ukpga/1983/20/section/2 and www.legislation.gov.uk/ukpga/1983/20/section/3

Chapter 24

1   Loewenstein, R.J. (2018) 'Dissociation debates: Everything you know is wrong.' *Dialogues in Clinical Neuroscience 20*, 3, 229–242. Accessed on 31/05/22 at: https://doi.org/10.31887/DCNS.2018.20.3/rloewenstein

2   Mind (2025) *How to get help in a crisis.* Accessed on 04/02/25 at: www.mind.org.uk/information-support/guides-to-support-and-services/crisis-services/getting-help-in-a-crisis

Chapter 25

1   Zawitz, R.X. (1981) Tangle Creations. Tangle, Inc. San Francisco.

Chapter 27

1   Reinders, A.A.T.S. and Veltman, D.J. (2021) 'Dissociative identity disorder: Out of the shadows at last?' *The British Journal of Psychiatry 210*, 413. Accessed on 09/02/25 at: www.cambridge.org/core/services/aop-cambridge-core/content/view/8E2884FA8669A9A64790E5C47AD72DC7/S0007125020001683a.pdf/dissociative-identity-disorder-out-of-the-shadows-at-last.pdf

Conclusion

1   Kastrup, B., Crabtree, A. and Kelly, E.F. (2018) 'Could multiple personality disorder explain life, the universe and everything?' *Scientific American.* Accessed on 28/06/25 at https://www.scientificamerican.com/blog/observations/could-multiple-personality-disorder-explain-life-the-universe-and-everything

DID and OSDD Dictionary of Terminology

1   NHS Dorset Neurodiversity Hub (2025) *Exploring Neurodiversity: What does neurotypical mean?* Accessed on 29/01/25 at: www.nhsdorset.nhs.uk/neurodiversity/explore

2   NHS Dorset Neurodiversity Hub (2025) *Exploring Neurodiversity: What is neurodiversity?* Accessed on 29/01/25 at: www.nhsdorset.nhs.uk/neurodiversity/explore

3   NHS Dorset Neurodiversity Hub (2025) *Exploring Neurodiversity: What does neurotypipcal mean?* Accessed on 29/01/25 at: www.nhsdorset.nhs.uk/neurodiversity/explore

4   Porges, S.W. (2011) *The Polyvagal Theory: Neurophysiological Foundations of Emotions, Attachment, Communication, and Self-Regulation.* New York: W.W. Norton & Company.

RAISING READERS
Books Build Bright Futures

Dear Reader,

We'd love your attention for one more page to tell you about the crisis in children's reading, and what we can all do.

Studies have shown that reading for fun is the **single biggest predictor of a child's future life chances** – more than family circumstance, parents' educational background or income. It improves academic results, mental health, wealth, communication skills, ambition and happiness.[1]

The number of children reading for fun is in rapid decline. Young people have a lot of competition for their time. In 2024, 1 in 10 children and young people in the UK aged 5 to 18 did not own a single book at home.[2]

Hachette works extensively with schools, libraries and literacy charities, but here are some ways we can all raise more readers:

- Reading to children for just 10 minutes a day makes a difference
- Don't give up if children aren't regular readers – there will be books for them!
- Visit bookshops and libraries to get recommendations
- Encourage them to listen to audiobooks
- Support school libraries
- Give books as gifts

There's a lot more information about how to encourage children to read on our website: **www.RaisingReaders.co.uk**

Thank you for reading.

hachette
UK

1   National Literacy Trust, 'Book Ownership in 2024', November 2024, https://literacytrust.org.uk/research-services/research-reports/book-ownership-in-2024
2   OECD, '21st-Century Readers: Developing Literacy Skills in a Digital World', OECD Publishing, Paris, 2021, https://www.oecd.org/en/publications/21st-century-readers_a83d84cb-en.html